At a time when most black Americans were relegated to service as cooks and stewards, the African-American crew of the USS *Mason* made history by escorting six convoys across the Atlantic, performing all the duties of seamanship needed to take a warship into combat. This is the story of their experiences as part of the U.S. Navy's tentative moves toward racial integration in the enlisted ranks during the war.

It is a collective memoir, compiled by best-selling author and Emmy-nominated filmmaker Mary Pat Kelly from extensive interviews with surviving crew members and new research in Navy records made public for the first time. Never before has the story of the *Mason* been told from the crew's point of view. They recall incidents of prejudice exhibited by other ships' crews and discrimination at most port calls, but mostly their story is a positive one that focuses on their highly successful shipboard experiences. They mastered all rates and skills, moving at accelerated paces from lowest to highest enlisted ranks, and proved they could perform combat duties as well as or better than white sailors.

In October 1944, during a fierce storm in the North Atlantic, they shepherded some twenty vessels to safety despite serious damage to their own ship. With the storm still raging, the crew braved forty-foot waves to weld together open seams in the *Mason*'s deck and to make other dangerous repairs before persisting in rejoining the convoy, while similar escorts sought out the safety of port. These actions earned the respect of many and the recommendation that a Letter of Commendation be included in each man's file—a recommendation that was not acted upon.

The men's candid comments about race relations both in the wartime Navy and American society at large contribute significantly to the social history of the United States as well as to the history of the U.S. Navy. A documentary on the men of the *Mason* has also been produced by the author for public television.

Proudly We Served

Proudly We Served

The Men of the USS *Mason*

Mary Pat Kelly

NAVAL INSTITUTE PRESS
Annapolis, Maryland

Library of Congress Cataloging-in-Publication Data

Kelly, Mary Pat.
  Proudly we served : the men of the USS Mason / Mary Pat Kelly.
      p.   cm.
  ISBN 1-55750-453-9 (alk. paper)
      1. USS Mason (Destroyer escort)   2. World War, 1939–1945—Naval
operations, American.   3. Afro-American seamen—History—20th
century.   4. United States—Armed Forces—History—20th century.
I. Title.
  D774.M36K45   1995
  940.54'5973—dc20   94-23820
                                                                              CIP

Printed in the United States of America on acid-free paper ∞

9 8 7 6 5 4 3 2

First printing

Unless otherwise noted, all photos are taken from the collection of James
W. Graham and are used with his permission.

Frontispiece: Silhouetted against their ship and the snow are 2 of the *Mason*'s
160 black enlisted crewmen on commissioning day, March 20, 1944.

To the men of the *Mason* and their families

Contents

Preface

In 1992 I was directing a documentary about the three hundred thousand American servicemen and women who served in the north of Ireland during World War II. Destroyer escort sailors played a significant part in this story. They had found a warm welcome and rest from the Battle of the Atlantic in the ports of Derry and Belfast and Bangor. Derry had been the headquarters for the destroyer escorts, and people there still remember the sailors fondly. I planned to feature these men in the documentary *Home Away from Home: The Yanks in Ireland.* Then Dr. Martin Davis, historian of the Destroyer Escort Sailors Association, gave me a newspaper clipping from 1944 written by the first black war correspondent to sail on a navy warship, Thomas W. Young. The headline read, "Irish First to Treat USS *Mason* Crew Like Real Americans." It seems Belfast had been the first port of call for the *Mason,* a destroyer escort manned by a predominantly black crew. The men were welcomed by people grateful to the American sailors who were keeping the vital supply lines open between Europe and North America. In the article Young quotes one sailor's reaction: "Funny how I had to come all the way across the ocean to a foreign country before I got to enjoy the feeling of being an American."

These black sailors were serving in a segregated navy, defending a country where segregation was the law in many states. According to Bill Bland, nicknamed "Half-Hitch" because of his propensity to fight anyone who criticized the *Mason:* "Here we were, all young. We were scared. We were coming from a country where we couldn't even go to the movie show in some places. We get to Ireland and the people call us Yanks. Not Tan Yanks like we were called in other places. Yanks. Just like they called the white sailors, and it was good." Young himself (as a widely traveled man from a privileged family) did not see Belfast as a world capital, but he understood the essence of the experience. He concluded the article: "We are now racing across the Atlantic again in the endless pursuit of German U-boats and memories of that last night in Ireland are fresh. . . . By now, I am completely persuaded that the men of the USS *Mason* enjoyed one of the great moments of their lives during their visit to Ireland. It was the people of that Northern Irish seaport who gave them that moment."

I decided then and there to interview these men for the documentary. It took James W. Graham, founder of the USS *Mason* Association, exactly twenty-four hours to assemble six members of the crew and arrange to meet me at the USS *Intrepid* Sea-Air-Space Museum, where an exhibit honoring the naval service of African Americans from the Revolutionary War period to the present was on display. This would be the first time the USS *Mason* story would be documented on film, and the veterans were ready. When I arrived an hour before the meeting was to begin, Bill Bland was waiting at the gate. He had driven down from Providence, Rhode Island. In fact, he had sneaked out of the house because at the time he was supposedly too ill to leave his bed, let alone make the drive to New York City. But he would not be deterred. He had come from a navy family and knew firsthand of the contributions that black sailors had made from the beginning. "My father was in the navy when it was coal and my grandfather when it was sail." When the *Mason* was commissioned Bland's grandfather came down to look her over. "It's a nice enough ship," he said, "but where are you going to hoist the sail when that motor breaks down?"

In the midst of filming, a school group from the South Bronx arrived. They were excited to meet the men whose photos were in the exhibit. As the children—particularly the boys—asked questions and the men answered, the importance of handing the *Mason* story to the next generation became concrete for me.

A few days later I received a letter. The crew of the *Mason* wanted me to write their book. My first question was, "Wouldn't you prefer to have a black writer, a naval historian?" But Graham wanted me. I think he had approached others, but there had been delays, and time lost meant shipmates lost. I would do. I had written another book. I had the academic credentials. I could listen. I could research. The crew were not interested in advancing any ideology or critical historical theory; they just wanted the story told. They were offering me an opportunity to join their circle and write down the tale.

Graham started me on my research. He sent me documents. I visited the National Archives. I attended the 1993 reunion and met more crew members. I visited homes and hospitals and, sadly, attended Bill Bland's funeral. Sometimes I felt Graham was like a Zen master sending me out to discover truths that he already knew. But the process was important, and near the end came the reward. We serendipitously discovered Professor Mansel Blackford, Captain Blackford's son, who had just taken possession of his father's papers. During the Christmas vacation of 1993 he sent packet upon packet of letters and documents that his father had saved. Among these was the official report on convoy NY-119, which contained information none of the men had known and which has never been published.

But more of that later. Time to go back to the beginning, when the world was aflame and the war was the crucible in which 160 young men were tried and tested. Their voices tell the tale.

Acknowledgments

All of us connected to the USS *Mason* wish to thank President William Jefferson Clinton. That's how he signed his name on the declaration he presented to the USS *Mason* Association at a ceremony held on September 16, 1994, to honor African American World War II veterans. The congressional black caucus had convened the ceremony, where Congressman Charles Rangel, a Korean War veteran, presided, assisted by Ron Armstead, a Vietnam War vet. President Clinton spoke specifically of Eleanor Roosevelt's efforts to open all ranks of the U.S. Navy to black sailors, and in acknowledging the pioneering work of the *Mason*'s crew, he crowned her efforts.

I would like to say thank you to the men of the *Mason* and their families for inviting me to play some part in their story. I am grateful for their guidance, support, and sustenance, especially the wonderful meals after every session. Which brings me to James Warren Graham and his wife, Barbara. Their faith and determination created this book. Lorenzo and Terry DuFau, and Gordon Buchanan, have joined them in devoting themselves to telling the *Mason*'s story.

The crew also found an early supporter in Dr. Martin Davis. I wish to thank him, as well as John Cosgrove, Art Filete, Sam Saylor, and the members of the Destroyer Escort Sailors Association, for their help in completing this project. Capt. William Blackford's presence was felt through his son Mansel Blackford and the entire Blackford family. Thank you, Manse.

I am grateful to the staff of the Naval Institute Press—especially Linda O'Doughda, Mary Lou Kenney, and Susan Artigiani—but my greatest appreciation must go to Mark Gatlin, whose energy and vision brought this book to life. The "luck of the *Mason*" led us to Capt. Eugene (Gene) Kendall, who by connecting the *Mason* crew members to the new generation of African American navy officers, confirmed the worth of all of their sacrifices. Thank you to Adm. Frank Kelso, Adm. Thomas Lynch, Adm. James Miller, Adm. Mac Gaston, and Adm. Bill Thompson, all of whom hosted the crew at various functions.

Special thanks to Edward Moraldo, Regina Akers, and Kathy Lloyd of the Naval Historical Center's operational archives branch and to Professor Morris MacGregor for the helpful suggestions. Similarly, the staff of the National Archives were most cooperative.

I want to thank those who helped me assemble this book. First, Willia Osby and William Francis Osby, who were always there. Then, Carol Forget, Ted Pankin, and, as always, Louise McKeown. Thank you to Jack Gallant, Carolyn Allison, Laura Freeman, and Lynn Kurkal of the U.S. Navy World War II Commemorative Committee. I appreciate the help of Steve Harris, Don Gold, Delores Edwards, Louis Cubillo, Eddie Panian, and my partners Oshun Mugwana and Onkiwa Bill Wallace in the production of the documentary that grew with this book.

I am grateful to Frank Price for his early encouragement on the feature film. Ian Henderson, David Boyce, Maebeth Fenton, Sheelagh Wylie, Gordon Glenn, and Stephen Doherty of the Northern Ireland Tourist Board have renewed the *Mason*'s Belfast connection in a very happy way. Bob Kline's wonderful prints enhanced the book.

My family has been supportive, as always, and I appreciate the interest too of Mary Gordon and Pat Hume. Always there is my husband, Martin Sheerin, who has had as much fun at the Graham household and the *Mason* reunions as I have. I appreciate the contribution his National Archives photographs make to the book, but his love and encouragement are truly beyond reckoning.

Proudly We Served

Prologue

Yeoman Mel Grant tapped out the terse sentences of the war diary: "Screening starboard bow as before. Wind and sea rising. Many breakdowns reported by small craft and increasing difficulty with tow wires. Some alarm noted in TBS transmission." The ship rolled again. He waited, clutching the table. "Some alarm"; *that* understated the case. Some alarm. They had spent the past thirty days trying to drag a convoy of unwieldy yard tugs, leaky barges, massive car floats, merchant ships, and the huge oiler *Maumee* across the Atlantic. Nineteenth-century sailing ships had made the passage in a week. The *Queen Mary* had passed them four times. The convoy was averaging less than five miles per hour. Any man on the ship could walk faster than that.

The USS *Mason*, with her four sister destroyer escorts (DEs), circled the slow-moving ships, prodding stragglers, patrolling their sectors, listening for the sonar contacts that could mean U-boats, keeping station, protecting their ungainly herd. The weather had been terrible, but that was the norm in the North Atlantic in mid-autumn: winds of twenty miles per hour, seas from ten to twenty feet. Then, on October 10, the velocity increased. Winds were thirty to forty miles per hour, and the crew measured gusts of ninety miles per hour. Seas ran at forty to fifty feet. Now the barges themselves became agents of destruction, swinging wildly from their tows, fraying the lines, dragging down the small craft that pulled against them. Two had capsized. The *Mason*'s crew joined the other DEs in the scramble to rescue the men trapped in the sinking ships. They pulled most of them aboard, but others went down to the sea bottom.

The men in the radio shack heard the screams of the men trapped aboard picked up by the TBS as they went down. The DEs themselves were in danger. Barely three hundred feet long, they were heavily armed but had been hastily constructed. They were "throwaway" ships designed to last long enough to escort a few convoys, seek out the subs, and, if necessary, take a torpedo to save a larger, more vital ship.

They had fought their way across three thousand miles of rampaging seas. All signs now pointed to worsening weather. In charge of the convoy, Comdr. Alfred Lind faced a decision. Should the convoy huddle together and try to ride out the storm as a unit, or should he detach the twenty small manned vessels and let them make for the "shelter of nearby land at their best speed"? He would be asking the small craft to struggle to shore without adequate escort protection or service vessels, but to keep the small ships at sea meant almost certain disaster. They could overturn, and in such seas how could he count on a successful rescue?

James Graham waited in the radio shack for the message that would reveal the commodore's decision. Meanwhile, in the wheelhouse, Charles Divers watched the inclinometer, which measured the degrees the ship rolled. Divers had heard other DE sailors brag about their ships taking forty-degree rolls; as he watched a huge wave hit, the inclinometer read seventy—seventy degrees! Ninety degrees was flat over. A DE couldn't come back from seventy. "We're not going to make it!" Divers thought. But the *Mason* held. She held and then lurched. Finally she came back up, water pouring down into the engine below decks. Albert Watkins and the rest of the "Black Gang" in the engine room struggled to cover their switchboard with canvas to keep the water from the electricity.

Lorenzo Dufau and Gordon Buchanan stood by their signal lights. Arnold Gordon manned the sonar equipment. Merwin Peters and Benjamin Garrison joined Graham in the radio shack. The message came. The *Mason* would form a new convoy with twenty vessels: the oilers and the independent tugs, plus the HMS *Pretext*, a Lend-Lease tender, and HMS *Astravel*, a Lend-Lease "A.P.C." (coastal transport). If the *Mason* could get these faster vessels to Plymouth safely and then return with ships from Plymouth to help the rest of the convoy bring in the tugs and barges, perhaps they all could reach a safe harbor.

On October 18 the *Mason* sighted Bishop Rock. The weather had gotten much worse. The wind increased to forty knots, with gusts of fifty. Still they pushed on, against the sea, shepherding their charges toward port. As the war diary reports, "Section began scattering badly with the danger that some vessels might be swept on past the harbor entrance." The *Mason* urgently requested assistance from local escorts. None came. The wind increased to sixty knots; visibility dropped to zero. "The HMS *Pretext* had no charts of Falmouth," the official navy report noted later, "so it was necessary to lead the section from buoy to buoy and between buoys and to run back to the end of the column about seven miles astern to guide in possible stragglers."

To do this Captain Blackford had to call on the engine room gang, on every seaman, and each member of the communications division. The whole crew mobilized as he increased speed to seventeen knots. Then, with the shoreline in sight, the deck of the *Mason* broke in two. A welded seam gave, and the deck came apart; then two reinforcing beams in one compartment collapsed. But men went on deck in the face of wind and waves and repaired the break. The *Mason* held together. A sailor's pride in his ship can be heard beneath the laconic words of the war diary: "The ship handled well at all times and showed little tendency to broach running before the seas which were by then quite high. Wind reached a maximum of seventy to eighty knots. . . . All vessels of the advance were successfully turned over to the local escort inside the bay at Falmouth by 1645. It was impossible to report this to C.T.G. (Commander Task Group) 27.5 at the time as the regular antennae had blown away and it was necessary to rig a new one."

They had made it. But no one relaxed. The crew took two hours to strengthen the weld in the deck, rig up a new antenna, and pump out the engine room. Then the *Mason* turned back into the wind and a still treacherous sea to aid the convoy that still floundered in the storm. Two British vessels, HMS *Rochester* and HMS *Saladin*, were ordered to accompany the DE. The three ships started together, but almost immediately the British stopped and returned to port. This action astonished the *Mason*'s crew.

The amazed signalmen DuFau and Buchanan received semaphore messages from the British ships. First, the Royal Navy sloops wanted to establish a chain of command. "They wanted to know if our captain had been commissioned before their captain!" DuFau remembers. Even when the U.S. captain's seniority was established, the British declined to follow the *Mason* into the open sea. The *Mason*'s war diary records a diplomatic response to the sloops. "Neither of the sloops able to make headway against the sea and returned shortly thereafter. This vessel able to make good headway. . . . No noticeable strain to our hull or engines . . . LT-653 located at 20:16 and given necessary instructions for entering port." The *Mason* stayed at sea for three more days, assisting twelve ships of the convoy.

She was ordered to shelter from another storm, but from October 24 to 27 she worked to salvage barges off the French coast.

In his official report to the chief of naval operations, Commander Lind wrote that he had directed the commanding officer of the *Mason* to take "any safe course" and even "turn back if he considered it advisable, but Captain Blackford insisted on going back to rejoin the convoy." Lind concluded, "CTG 27.5 considers the performance of the USS *Mason,* her Commanding Officer, officers and men outstanding and recommends that this ship be given a letter of commendation to be filed in the record of each officer and man on board that vessel." The other DEs in NY-119 also performed bravely, but only the crew of the *Mason* was recommended for individual commendation. Receiving such an honor would have been a high point for the crew and front-page news in papers throughout the black community. U.S. "Negro Bluejacket Heroes" the headlines would have read. What a moment to savor.

But the moment never happened. The commendations never came. The crew never even knew they had been recommended for honors by the convoy commander. Their own Captain Blackford had posted on the ship bulletin board *his* recommendation that they be commended. But the navy never responded to him. There were no commendations, no headlines. In fact, when the crew finally were granted liberty and headed for the USO in Plymouth, England, where rumor had it they were serving hot dogs, mustard, and Coca Cola, they were turned away. Whites only.

Here in a nutshell is the story of the USS *Mason.* At sea the crew were trained technicians manning a sophisticated warship, following the captain they respected. Maybe convoy escort duty was not the most glamorous the navy could offer, but the Battle of the Atlantic could not have been won without the DEs. In his memoirs Winston Churchill wrote, "The only thing I really feared during the war was the U-boat." If the fragile lifeline of merchant ships and Lend-Lease vessels that linked Britain to the United States had broken, Britain would have had to surrender. From 1939 to 1941 the U-boats dominated the sea. The German subs sank merchant ships one mile outside of New York harbor. The destroyer escorts of the U.S. Navy and Coast Guard, together with the Royal Navy, became a crucial factor in the antisubmarine effort.

The *Mason* joined the band of more than five hundred small maneuverable ships pledged to guard the convoys, even to place themselves between a torpedo and a larger ship. But when it was time for rewards to be given—be it letters of commendation or hot dogs and Coke—the reply was, "Whites only." Even today, few people know of the *Mason.* Why did the navy itself play down the achievements of this predominately black ship? And, most importantly, who were these young men—the first and then the forgotten?

Signing Up

"I guess they're going to let us into this war after all," James Graham remembers thinking as the call for black recruits went out in the days following the air raid on Pearl Harbor. Black men had fought in every one of America's wars in spite of the contradiction inherent in defending a country that first enslaved them and then denied them their most basic rights. Each time, as soon as peace came, their contribution was forgotten. Jack Foner, in his 1974 study *Blacks and the Military in American History: A New Perspective,* reminded the nation that thousands of black men fought in the Revolutionary War; 186,000 were soldiers in the Civil War; and 30,000 black sailors made up 30 percent of the Union Navy's enlisted personnel. They served as seamen, performing all shipboard duties. The identities of most of the thousands of African Americans who took part in the navy's battles at sea are not recorded. There are no monuments to the men who piloted coastal vessels, manned guns, and worked the sails. Only a few stories of the bravery and skill of these men have been preserved.

One of the best documented is that of Capt. Robert Smalls. Smalls and six other slaves were part of the crew on a Confederate gunboat, the *Planter,* in Charleston, South Carolina. With their minds set on freedom, they plotted to commandeer the ship and turn her over to the Union Navy. On a night when the officers and some of the white crew were ashore, they overpowered the remaining crew. (Smalls and the others had already smuggled their families on board.) Now they hoisted the stars and bars and sailed out of Charleston harbor. Somehow they convinced the authorities that they were off on patrol.

Sailing upriver toward the Union Navy they risked attack from the Yankees. Did they run up the stars and stripes or a white flag of surrender? Or did one of their men use semaphores to signal to the other ship their true identity or intentions? However it happened, Capt. Robert Smalls and his crew were welcomed into the fleet. He was decorated by President Lincoln himself, commissioned a captain in the U.S. Navy, and placed in command of the ship he had captured. But his rank was an army designation since the navy had no black officers. Nevertheless, Smalls remained a seafarer all his life. He went on to fight for the Union, and after the war he was elected to the House of Representatives for six terms during the years of Reconstruction. A stellar life, yet even such a dramatic story is little known.

In the years following Reconstruction the contributions of black soldiers and sailors were forgotten, and the political achievements of men like Robert Smalls were tainted by a rewriting of the events by those determined to wrest back any power achieved by black citizens.

In D. W. Griffith's *Birth of a Nation*, legislators such as Robert Smalls are portrayed as buffoons lounging in the legislative chamber, feet up on their desks, chomping on chicken legs. In the film, the Ku Klux Klan becomes a noble brotherhood dedicated to reclaiming southern honor. Woodrow Wilson showed *Birth of a Nation* at the White House and called it "History writ with lightning." This is the context within which all black sailors were discharged from the seaman's ranks of the navy. The "Great White Fleet" found room for only four hundred black men, all of whom were required to serve as cooks and waiters. Further enlistment was closed to black Americans. If one of Robert Smalls's sons, perhaps one who had been part of the adventure in Charleston harbor, had followed his father into the navy, he would have been ejected in 1900. If one of Smalls's grandsons had sought to enlist, he would have been refused entry. Suppose he had said, "But my grandfather was a naval hero—decorated by the president, made the captain of a fighting ship. I deserve a place." He would have been told "The military reflects society. It is not up to the services to solve social problems."

On the eve of America's entrance into World War II, Civil Rights leaders such as Walter White of the NAACP, A. Philip Randolph, Adam Clayton Powell, Jr., Mary McLeod Bethune, and Dr. Marjorie Stewart Joyner saw the needs of the military as an opportunity. "If our sons were going to fight for the freedom of people abroad then we expected some attention to be paid to our struggles here at home,"

Dr. Joyner recalled in a recent interview for this book. Now ninety-seven years old and still an activist, she worked closely with educator Mary McLeod Bethune and Eleanor Roosevelt on Civil Rights issues. The black community saw the first lady as their liaison with the power structure. Again and again Mrs. Roosevelt had risked vilification to support the cause of equality and justice. The furor caused by her smallest gestures reveals the depth of the country's racism and the "go slow" policy of even progressive whites. Joseph Lash, in *Eleanor and Franklin,* cites incident after incident of angry calls to the White House. Just the rumor that Mrs. Roosevelt had ridden in an open car with a black woman in Georgia stirred protest. When, at her urging, Franklin Roosevelt met with Walter White and other black leaders to discuss a wider role for black men in the military, it was seen as more of Eleanor's meddling. Lash reports the outcome.

The conference took place in September 1941. At that time, black men were serving in the segregated army but mostly in support and supply units that were not allowed in combat. There were a few black army officers, but no African Americans could join the Army Air Corps. The navy was virtually for whites only, justifying the exclusion by pointing out how difficult it would be to segregate crews in the close quarters of a ship. The president accepted this rationale; indeed, he refused to push the military. When the Civil Rights leaders tried to point out how much of the military's policy was based on racial stereotyping and an unquestioned assumption of black inferiority, they met a wall of indifference. Secretary of War Henry L. Stimson would later write in his diary that his representative at the meeting found Roosevelt's "gymnastics as to politics a rather amusing affair."

The military assumed that Roosevelt simply wanted to appear "to appease Negro politicians who are trying to get the Army committed to Negro officers." Stimson then casually repeats an old slander about "colored officers" in several of the divisions that went over to France in World War I. "The poor fellows made perfect fools of themselves." Actually, the black troops in combat in France had distinguished themselves, and many had been decorated by the French government. One regiment, the 368th Infantry, was accorded "the honor of the victory of Benarville" by a French commander, only to become the victim of demeaning rumors spread by U.S. Army personnel. The famed 369th regiment received the Croix de Guerre. When accusations against the black soldiers began to surface, then-Secretary of War, Newton T. Baker, instituted an investigation and found that "there was no basis at all for the general assumptions with regard to the action of colored troops in this battle and elsewhere in France."

Pearl Harbor and America's entry into the war made increased military manpower crucial. Black political and church leaders also stepped up the pressure, and some changes began. The navy opened its ranks to general black enlistment on June 1, 1942. They set up a segregated facility at Great Lakes Naval Training Center named, appropriately, if ironically, Camp Robert Smalls. But even then, if Captain Smalls's great grandson had been one of the enlistees, he still would have been shunted off to become a steward. As late as February 1943, 98 percent of those serving in the U.S. Navy were white. Of the 26,909 black sailors, 19,227 were in the stewards branch, 2,020 were Seabees, and only 6,662 had been accepted into the general service.* Though a small number of the men went on for advanced training, most were sent to shore stations as unskilled labor.

The navy registered surprise at the initial lack of enthusiasm for naval service among young black men. The official navy report attributed this to "Negroes' relative unfamiliarity with the sea or the large inland lakes and their consequent fear of water" (54). No reports discussed the real fears—the white fears generated by racism. The navy did not think white sailors would accept black sailors as their equals (see Appendix A). African Americans knew where the navy wanted them—in the kitchen!

Word had gone out in the black community, however, that the navy was now opening its ranks. Not that Robert Smalls's great-grandson could ever hope to captain a ship as his ancestor had. There were no plans to have black commissioned officers, but the navy would train him to become a petty officer, the equivalent of the army's noncom. He might even make chief petty officer, a position similar to the army's top sergeant. The navy was still segregated, but here was an opportunity, and this attracted the young men who would become the crew of the USS *Mason.* They did not know as they entered the recruiter's office in Charleston, Cleveland, New Orleans, Kansas City, and New York that of all the more than one hundred thousand black men who would serve in the navy in World War II, only they—the 160 men of the *Mason*—would actually take

* These and other cited facts and observations are taken from "The Negro in the Navy" (a first draft narrative), prepared by the Historical Section, Bureau of Naval Personnel (1947).

a warship into battle. Only they would prove their seamanship by crossing the Atlantic eight times as convoy escorts.

Fifty years later the men still remember those missions. The deck log, the war diary of the *Mason*, task force records, and the navy's studies of "the Negro sailor" provide a context for their reminiscences. The men remember the difficulties: the battles with white sailors from other ships who dared insult the *Mason*, the indignities suffered in segregated ports, their feeling that the *Mason* was an experiment the navy hoped would fail. But their most vivid memories are of being young and strong, confident in their abilities and sure of their accomplishments. The title they chose for the book expresses their conviction—*Proudly We Served.*

Here they are to tell their story. First, James Warren Graham— tall, well built, an athlete. Not much of a talker, but he laughs from a place so deep down inside of him that it is clear he keeps whole parts of himself below the surface. Anger can erupt from those depths, but most of the time he prefers to be what he appears, a big, good-looking man, confident and easygoing.

James W. Graham: I was born in a little place called Lake City, South Carolina. I think the population was under ten thousand. My mother died when I was seven, eight, or nine—I don't remember—and I went to live with my sister and brother-in- law in Darlington, South Carolina. He was a schoolteacher and a graduate of Morehouse College in Atlanta, Georgia. I admired him. As a matter of fact, he was my first hero.

When I first met him, my sister was in college, and they were going together. I egged her on to marry him because he was a handsome man, well educated, and he spoke beautifully. I fell in love with him too. I wanted to be like him. I played football, basketball, and he wanted to get a scholarship for me to attend Morehouse College. But then the war got in the way.

I remember the day I went down to Charleston to enlist. I went with other members of the junior class. We wanted to become pilots—about five of us—but the recruiter told us point blank that Negroes couldn't serve in the air corps. Coming back home, we saw a navy recruiting officer. He called us in and said, "Why don't you go into the navy?"

I said, "No, I'm not going to cook for anybody or clean up behind anybody."

"You don't have to go into that. You can join the seaman branch the same as the white guys, the white sailors."

So I said, "Okay." But then you had to be eighteen or something, I think, before you could enlist. And I said, "Well, I'm not eighteen; I'm seventeen," or whatever.

"Well, put your age up a year," he said. So I put down eighteen!

I got home and my brother-in-law had a *fit*. He showed me hell. My sister always could calm him down, but this time he was upset something terrible. He could have kept me out of the army because being a schoolteacher in a southern town, he had influence with the powers that be, put it that way. And he had it fixed up that I wouldn't have to be in the army; I'd get a deferment. And when I told him I had enlisted in the navy, he had a fit!

But in the end, he was very proud of me, and he bragged about me a lot. At that time he had two children, and I was his third son. He'd tease me, "Don't you want to change your name to McIver?" That was his name—McIver. Because of him and the way I was raised, I knew I could do any job in the navy as well as anybody else. I was brought up, to tell you the truth, with a superiority complex.

Gordon Buchanan is a quick moving, fast-talking man with a mind-driven body that does not rest long enough to acquire much fat or worry too much about yesterday. When Buchanan talks he leans forward, gesturing, acting out the part, grabbing at new knowledge. He's called Skinny or "Noo Yawk," the title he wrote on his sailor's jacket.

Gordon "Skinny" Buchanan: I was born in Harlem. We moved out to Corona, Long Island, early on when I was about six or seven years old. I've been out on Long Island all these years. It was completely different from Harlem. There were a small number of blacks there, so I went to school with all white kids in those days. In fact, when I went to high school, I was one of three blacks in the whole school. I got a very good education in that school. I studied German. In fact, when I was aboard the *Mason*, I was part of the German prize crew because of my knowledge of German. If any German ship had surrendered to us, I would be one of the ones that would go aboard to bring it back to the United States.

Growing up, my hobby was building model planes and ships. Just before the war, I got in the habit of stopping by the big public library we had here in Jamaica on my way home from school and looking up in *Jane's Fighting Ships* pictures of all the ships. I'd make my little drawings, take all the information down, go home, draw it up to scale, and then I would build it.

When the war began, in December 1941, I had over two hundred models of ships. I just loved the ships. By March 1942 I was working downtown as a delivery boy, and I would see the ships in New York harbor, because the war had just begun. I first tried to enlist in March. I just *had* to get in the navy, with all these ships. Oh, that's all I wanted to do, go to sea. Here I was living in New York, and I had to go to sea. But I didn't get in that March, when I wanted to get in.

I had no idea that if I'd have gone in at that time, I would have been a steward. And I don't think I could have handled that. It would have been just too much for me. I would have done something desperate. I just don't know what it would have been. I didn't understand what blacks were doing in the navy. I was just going to join up to fight for the country. That was in my head. I was a patriot.

But I had to wait until the end of the summer before I got in. The navy was changing; directives were coming down to open all ranks to blacks. They needed people to fight in the war. Don't forget, in '42, at the beginning of '42, the Japanese were just wiping us out all *over* the Pacific. In the Battle of the Atlantic, the German submarines, instead of staying over on the European side, were coming up and down the U.S. coast! So I understood that part. But I didn't know the different way blacks were treated in the navy.

So when I went in, I didn't know what I was in for, because I was born and raised in New York. I had no idea of this color line or anything like that. And I went downtown to get in the group. They had about 250 white sailors down there, and about fifteen to eighteen of us black sailors.

And they said that they wanted us to swear in. Swearing-in time came, and the very first thing they said was, "All you Coloreds over there in the back." That was the first day I had ever heard that, and I started thinking, "What is *this*? No, something's wrong here." So when they started the swearing-in ceremony, I *mouthed* it, I was so mad at the way they'd separated me from the group. I had been mixed in with everybody else. I didn't know any better.

But when we boarded the train, the troop train to Chicago, I was riding Pullman service. I had a bed all night, and all those white sailors were sitting up in the coach. And I said, "Well, maybe this ain't so bad. This just might be all right."

Lorenzo DuFau was a little older when he enlisted. He was married and a father. He has a philosophic turn of mind. Manners matter to him. He has been raised to be courteous, almost courtly. He remembers as a boy walking streets so dark you could not see whether the wide, recessed porches contained neighbors fanning themselves against the hot Louisiana night or if they were empty. "I said 'Good evening' anyway," he remembers. You had to "Hello the porch" because if you passed without greeting the people, you heard about it, or worse, your mother heard about it. White-bearded DuFau, a southern gentleman despite a lifetime in New York, is still ready to extend himself even if the porch is empty.

Lorenzo DuFau: Personally, I felt responsible as an American citizen *first*. I had a wife and kid down in New Orleans. I had a 3-A classification, so I was not going to be drafted. But once the navy announced they were opening the doors for us—that they were going to give rates—I decided to enlist. A recruiting officer in New Orleans who knew me personally, knew my family, tried to discourage me from volunteering. I said I wanted to, but he said, "You've got a 3-A classification; you don't have to worry for awhile." But I was determined.

I had a young son (he wasn't two years old at that time), and I felt if I could get into the service and do good, it would be an opening for him and others like him. It's just inbred in a man to want his child to be a little better off than he. That was one thing.

Also at that time I was hearing in the news about what was happening over in Germany with the repression that was going on, the terrible actions against the Jews. I heard about that through the newspapers. And I said, I can kill two birds with one stone. I could take part in trying to stop this action and also open doors here at home. It was a twofold thing. But I guess some people would look at me as being kind of stupid at that time, thinking I was young and foolish to get all patriotic, knowing what ordeals I was living under. But it was *my* home being violated, threatened, and I felt it was only right to defend it. A man will go forth and *defend* his home. You defend your family—you defend your country—because there's no other place that's home but here in America.

But times were tough then. Jobs . . . When I got married, believe it or not, I didn't have a regular job. The day I got married, I worked on a golf course, carrying a golf bag—I was a caddie. I think I made seventy-five cents for carrying a bag eighteen holes. That seventy-five cents made up the amount that I had to pay the minister for marrying me. I think the total was about three dollars. My mother-in-law, for our reception, had some cookies and lemonade. That was our wedding celebration!

I got a job working at a drugstore, delivering for a drugstore. I was making three dollars and seventy-five cents *a week*, working four o'clock until ten o'clock at night. And if you worked from eight o'clock until four o'clock in the daytime, you made four dollars and twenty-five cents a week.

But then I got a job as a mess attendant for the nurses in an army hospital. I was making about ninety dollars a month, which was pretty good, and it was civil service. As I said, I was classified 3-A at that time, because I had a wife and kid, so no draft was involved.

The Louisiana Weekly, a local black newspaper, announced that the navy was going to open up for rates; they were going to have rates other than mess attendants. I had always felt some type of a desire to be a part of something because, as I said, it's natural for a man to defend his home, when his family is threatened. Even under those conditions I still felt, "I'm defending my home." If somebody attacked our country, it's home to me. I have the right to do it. I feel obligated to do it.

The recruiter was a black fellow who had made chief petty officer. (He used to be a local singer. He had a beautiful bass voice.) When they announced the opening for rates, I said, "Well, this will be a good chance, if the right people get in, to open the door, and maybe when my son grows up things will be much better." Because things were real bad at that time. It was real bad.

For example, riding on the trolley, you had what they called a screen: a little barrier that they used to put up and you had to sit behind. They still have the trolley there. I love to ride the trolley when I go back home now, because you can sit anywhere. It's a wonderful place now, a wonderful place. That little board they put up there said, "Colored Patrons," and you'd move it back and forth depending on how many passengers. You'd sit behind that. There used to be incidents about that thing because some people used to really just flop you out of your seat even if you were sitting way back. I said, "Well, maybe if I get in the service, it will be a chance to open doors. Things will be better."

I wanted to prove my abilities and to get my kid from under that influence. But this recruiting officer resisted. He kept saying, "Are you sure you want to do this?" I said, "This is the chance to get my family away from New Orleans, and get my son out of here." I was determined not to raise him under that. So it was an opportunity to serve my country, open the doors for the black man in the navy, and get my family out of the South.

Charlie Divers always seems to be sizing things up. Born and brought up in Maywood, Illinois, a suburban black community, he had always been competent and confident and has a Chicagoan's delight in being in the know. When Oshun Mugwana, a Chicago film producer, and I went to interview him, we had a flat tire on the way to Divers's house. Divers took us to a used tire store where they deferred to him and gave us a special price because he used to inspect the boiler when he was the town engineer of Maywood.

Charles Divers: Well, I was born in Chicago, February 8, 1922. I graduated from Proviso High School, Maywood, Illinois. I worked several jobs in heating and air-conditioning in '39, '40, '41, until the Buick company opened a defense plant in Melrose Park, Illinois, and I was fortunate enough to get a job in there for seventy-five cents an hour. At that time that was very good money.

I signed up with the draft when the twenty-year olds were eligible. But then when I found out I was being groomed to go into the army, I volunteered for the navy.

I had had the experience of being in the CCC, the Civilian Conservation Corps, where we worked in reforesting. It was one of the government programs established during the Depression. I found out there about sleeping on the ground, and that wasn't my idea of the way to spend the war! So I opted for the navy, where we slept between clean sheets practically every night and got three hot squares a day, under most conditions.

Merwin Peters has no wrinkles, is all muscles, and barely looks fifty. Yet he is seventy and has survived total physical paralysis and great emotional distress. He sails in Alaska, and he and his wife still plan to take their boat around the world.

Merwin Peters: I was born and raised in Cleveland, Ohio. I was in high school at the time the war started. My dad had been in World War I as an enlisted army man, and all my growing up time, all I used to hear from him was, "If you were in the army, you wouldn't do this" or "If you were in the army, you wouldn't do that." After hearing that for some seventeen years, I decided I would *never* be in the army. When I learned that there was going to be a draft and that sooner or later I was going to be drafted, I decided that the army was not going to get me. As a matter of fact, I wasn't going to go *anywhere* where you had to do any marching or walking around a lot.

So I tried to enlist in the navy. At first I couldn't get in, so I tried the merchant marine. The merchant marine had a waiting list as long as your arm, and I couldn't get in that. So I opted to wait to enlist in the navy. I got on a waiting list, and eventually I was called. So I avoided the draft that way and got into the service that I wanted to get into.

Albert Watkins is the oldest of the crew members. Another Chicagoan, he is an insider, connected to a network of leaders in the community who always wore suits and elegant shoes and knew which precincts were important. Yet on the *Mason* he'd been down in the engine room. He opened a bottle of French wine for us as he explained the first steps that led him to join the Black Gang and to become the "oil king."

Albert Watkins: I had a minister who said he wasn't going to let me go because I had a wife. But, they had drafted us, and I had to go downtown. Sometimes the recruiters would play tricks on you. The guy would ask, "What branch of the service do you choose?" You'd choose one, and he'd say "All right," but he'd stamp something different on your hand. I said, "The navy!" and he stamped "navy" on top there. So it worked out. I went into the navy.

Benjamin Garrison radiates a certain authority that is obvious even if you did not know he had been a minister and a corrections officer all his life. He measures his words, even using parentheses when his listener needs further explanation. But he can joke at his own expense, and every once in awhile he lets something of his younger pre-pastoral self show.

Benjamin Garrison: After I graduated from high school, I worked for the army for two years on a base in Columbia, South Carolina. But I didn't like the monotony of the army. I thought that if I went into the army, I'd stay in one place, and I didn't want that. I wanted to travel and see things. I thought the navy would give me a better opportunity to do that, so I went to enlist in the navy. I'm glad that I met the recruiter that I did because he told me to come back six weeks later. At that point, blacks would be able to come in on an equal basis with anybody else. He said if I went in sooner I would be a member of the Seabees, which was a construction battalion, or a steward's mate. When he described what my other option was, I decided to wait and take that.

Before that, black people could serve only in the food services; there was absolutely no chance to enter on an equal basis with whites. But as a result of Mrs. Eleanor Roosevelt's agitation, when she joined with leaders like Congressman Adam Clayton Powell, Jr., and leaders of church groups, black people got into the services. They thought we could do the job.

I think one of the main problems with blacks coming into the service at that time was that blacks and whites had to sleep together and eat together, and I think a lot of people didn't want that to happen. That's one of the things that prevented us from going in on an equal basis at the beginning.

I grew up in South Carolina, and in my own life, almost everything was segregated: waiting rooms at the train stations, bus stations, drinking fountains, theaters. On all the buses you had to sit in the back; in trains you sat in the front. And if you went to a restaurant, you couldn't go in and order a meal like anyone else; you had to go to the back, and they'd give you a meal in a paper bag.

But you know, it's strange. I didn't realize until later how this should not be. When you're living in a situation and involved with school and work, you just don't realize. You can be in your own world, so to speak. And that's the way it was with me. I didn't really realize how it shouldn't be until I went into the service. Then I realized that this shouldn't be like it was.

Arnold Gordon is prickly and proud. Always aware that he does not look like a black man, he calls into question, rightly, the whole notion of ethnicity and the fallacy of race as a concept. He is writing his own book on the *Mason* and was both eager and reluctant to participate in this project.

Arnold Gordon: I was born in Chicago. My family was large; there were nine of us children, and we were very poor. When I was eight, my mother decided to move us to Michigan, about 125 miles from Chicago, so that we could live in a rural climate. My parents were both from the farm, in Mississippi, and they knew how to raise crops. It was in the Depression, so they took us up to the country where we could raise our own food, and that way we could survive. Nine kids was too many to be raising in a place like Chicago.

So I grew up in Bangor, Michigan, and joined the navy from Bangor. I had fallen for the advertisements about "Join the Navy and See the World," and I was extremely impressed by the fact that navy sailors scrubbed down their ships every morning and that they all wore clean white uniforms. To wear new or clean *anything* was a rare treat to me. So I looked forward to being in the navy because it was so clean. Four days before I was eighteen, I finally talked my mother into signing for me to join the navy, and I went back to Chicago to join.

In Michigan we were not in a segregated environment because there were not enough people of color in the area. There was prejudiced treatment from various people, but I was able to put up with it. It was a problem, but it was not like segregation in the South. There were only two of us in the whole school, and there were only two other black families in town. We were treated with prejudice and disrespect, but we took that in stride.

When I went in the navy, I never thought anything about race because of the way I was raised. I went into the recruiting office, and they immediately took me in. I was sworn in and went through the physical. I was among a lot of recruits—and all of them were white. We were all in this examining room in the nude, and we were going from doctor to doctor taking various tests. We were given papers to fill out. One of these papers asked us to list our ancestry. And so, not being aware of or thinking about prejudice or race or anything like that, I just put down my ancestry—"German, Irish, Indian, and Negro"—in the percentage order.

We went through the line. They were testing us, examining each entry. Each guy would examine a different part of the papers. We came to this one guy, and he was studying my papers. All of a sudden, he looked up and glared at me. He had a real frown on his face, and he examined me very carefully. Then he reached over and he got out a red pen. He wrote on the front of my jacket in over-an-inch-high letters, "Negro." I was immediately ushered out of the group of white sailors and put into a group of black sailors. Then I was sent to Great Lakes and put into a segregated camp.

Needless to say, I was scared to death. I had never been around that many black people in all my life! But I soon accepted it. I was used to being treated with prejudice. I didn't consider myself any different than anybody else. I made friends just like you would anywhere else. That's how I got into the black navy.

Mel Grant was a dining car waiter on the Union Pacific when he joined the army. He had been reluctant to leave the troop trains and "beaucoup" money he was making "supplying soldiers whatever." He told his story of being a slick operator while his little granddaughter snuggled up in his lap.

Mel Grant: I volunteered for the navy in 1942. I got a letter from Uncle Sam: "Greetings from the President of the United States of America. You have been accepted in the United States Army. Report for induction Saturday morning, 6 A.M., September 6, 1942." (I've got the letter at home on my old-time radio.) That's it. I had a 1-A card. I was from Kansas City, Kansas. All my friends from Kansas City who were in the army were going to Camp Shelby, Mississippi, and I wanted no part of Camp Shelby, no part of *Mississippi*, in 1942. I was a waiter on the Union Pacific, and I was making *mucho* money. "Beaucoup l'argent!"

I was a twenty-year-old guy living in Ogden, Utah, making money. See, the trains picked soldiers up in Ogden and took them out to Frisco or Los Angeles. They'd take the boat and go over and fight the Japs. So we had soldiers, five hundred at a time. We made all type of money waiting tables for these soldiers—all kinds of opportunities!

When the army called, I went right over to volunteer for the navy. This white fellow, a third-class yeoman, said, "What can I do for you?" Now, this was a Monday morning; by Saturday morning, 6 A.M., I had to be in the United States Army.

"I want to volunteer to join the navy right now!" I knew I had—what?—five days.

"What's your hurry?" he asked.

I said, "Look, man. I'm patriotic." It wasn't patriotism; I just wanted to avoid the army, Camp Shelby, Mississippi. I didn't want any part of that.

Before that time a black man could be only a mess attendant or a cook. Right? So when this white yeoman asked "What's the hurry?" I told him, "I'm patriotic, and I want to join the navy right now. Not tomorrow. Today!" Then I asked him point blank, "Look, can I get in or not?"

"What do you want to be? A cook?"

"No, man. Don't you know that I can try for any rate now? President Roosevelt changed things. That's the only reason I'm here. I know I don't want to be a cook. I don't cook for myself. I want to be a seaman, and go from there."

He said, "All right, all right."

I said, "Wait a second, now. Can you get me in the navy before Saturday?" He must have known that something was wrong, right?

"Well, I'll try. I'll try. I'll tell you what. Come back Tuesday for the blood test. Wednesday you've got to have . . ." something else, right? He told me, "We're trying to get about three hundred guys to volunteer at the same time so we can have one mass induction, one mass swearing-in."

So on Thursday afternoon, 2 P.M., there we all were. Most of the guys were doing the same thing I was, volunteering for the navy to avoid the army. They had gotten their greetings too. All these guys came in this room. There were about three hundred. I was the first one in that room because I've only got, now, until Saturday morning. I heard, "All of you raise your right hand." My hand went up first, and I was a navy man.

Then I took off and went down to Shreveport, Louisiana, to see my grandmother. I was raised in Louisiana. See, my mother died when I was less than two years old, so my grandmother raised me. I went down to see her because they gave me a week before I had to report to Great Lakes, Illinois—a week from that Thursday. Saturday morning at 6:30 A.M. two FBI agents were at my father's house in Kansas City, Kansas, looking for me. They thought I was a draft dodger. And my father said, "No, my son joined the navy, Thursday." They couldn't do anything. That's how close I missed Camp Shelby, Mississippi!

Winfrey Roberts joined the *Mason* on her third convoy. He takes pride in the skill of the engineering gang and the discipline that prepared him for a lifetime on the South Orange, New Jersey, police force.

Winfrey Roberts: I was born in North Carolina of a very illustrious family. My grandfather was postmaster for the town of Rich Square, and his brother was the registrar of deeds. That was around 1868.

My family moved when I was three years old to South Orange, New Jersey. (I still reside there. In fact, I live two blocks from where I started kindergarten.) I left South Orange when I was seventeen to go to Washington, D.C., just four months before I was supposed to graduate from high school. I promised my father I'd go to night school and finish. I went down to get one of those profitable government jobs that were available because of the war. I had two first cousins who lived in Washington who were the same age as I was and were also seniors in high school. They also dropped out of school and took the civil service exam, and we all went to work for the war department on the same day. I had volunteered for the coast guard, but I was turned down and then inducted into the navy.

Each man came to the navy from a different place—geographically, personally, and socially. But differences would be set aside as the men headed for the Great Lakes Naval Training Center and boot camp.

Boots

For many of the men the trip to Great Lakes Naval Training Center marked their first time away from home. Those who lived in the segregated South relished the change they would find up North and were disappointed to find Jim Crow waiting for them there. Their facility, Camp Robert Smalls, was segregated and separated from the main base by railroad tracks. The sailors at Camp Robert Smalls were as diverse in background and experience as their white counterparts in the main camp, though the navy establishment saw them as a monolithic group. Like all World War II veterans, the crew of the *Mason* found that basic training brought them into contact with men they never would have encountered otherwise. But at Great Lakes, civilian distinctions fell away in one general identification: they were all boots. Country boy or city slicker, each one was a beginner.

DuFau: There were three of us traveling from New Orleans to Chicago, Illinois. The personnel officer from the navy came aboard to check our reservations. They had reserved a roomette for us to sleep in. The officer instructed the conductor to see that we got our meals. Everything was paid for.

 We ate in the dining car. This was the first time I ever ate in the dining car. When we went up for breakfast in the dining car, this lady asked her husband, very loudly, "What are *they* doing up here?" He whispered that we were going into the service, and she sat quiet. It was an exciting thing for me to be there eating in that dining car. Walking through the train, going to our roomette, we'd get these strange looks. "What are *you* doing in that section?" But we arrived in Chicago with no incidents.

When we got to Great Lakes, it was late at night, and we didn't get any food. The next morning was a Saturday, the first morning we woke up on the base. We had the darndest breakfast I ever had. They gave us baked beans, corned beef, cornbread, and coffee. That was *breakfast,* my first meal in the navy! But once I got into it, I really loved it. In fact, you'd get to know the day of the week by the meals. They'd repeat the meals according to the day, so you could wake up any day of the week and know what meal it was.

Peters: I was inducted into the navy in Cleveland, Ohio, and went from there to Great Lakes, to Camp Robert Smalls, where I went through my boot camp training and then, after boot camp, to service school, where I specialized in radio communications.*

At that time the navy was segregated. I was fortunate, though, to go into the seaman branch of the navy, as opposed to being in the steward's branch. Still, Robert Smalls was a segregated camp. It was the only camp out of all the other camps that were at Great Lakes where black sailors were being trained at the time.

The conditions were good. Most of our company commanders were white naval enlisted men, but there were a few blacks. We were pretty much on our own—as I said, segregated—which meant that everything that went on in Camp Robert Smalls had to do with Camp Robert Smalls. We were ostracized from the rest of Great Lakes, and Great Lakes was a big training center at the time. The conditions under which we lived and worked were not bad, though.

I grew up in mixed neighborhoods, went to mixed schools, so this was a little bit strange to me, to be in a camp where all you had were black enlisted people, with white officers or white senior enlisted people over us. It wasn't easy.

Some of the whites were condescending. Having black enlisted navy men who were not stewards was a new thing for them. It took some time for them to become accustomed to it. But I can't say that I had any bad feelings about Great Lakes. I was happy to be doing what I was doing.

Roberts: I was one of a group of five who were the first inductees into the navy from Washington, D.C. Among the five there was

---

* Those who scored well on aptitude tests and had good records in boot camp were sent to service school. Most attended classes right at Robert Smalls.

one fellow who was older than we were. He was the valet for President Roosevelt. His name was Fields. He was very nice. We all liked him. As I got to know him he told me a lot of stories about his experiences in the White House. He was a real storyteller. I'm not going to repeat what he told me because I promised him that I wouldn't, so I won't.

We had a club car all to ourselves going from Washington, D.C., to Great Lakes. I thought maybe that was because the president's valet was with us. This was around February 1943, and Great Lakes was cold as the devil. I had heard that Chicago was the Windy City, but when I got off the train I thought the wind was going to blow me away!

The camp at Great Lakes was segregated, but that didn't surprise me. I had spent a year in Washington, D.C., before I went into the service, and I knew what segregation was. I couldn't sit down and eat a hot dog at a drugstore soda fountain there— and that was in the nation's capital! Once my cousin and I were walking home from work, and this policeman comes along swinging his billy club at us—for no reason!

I felt grateful I had grown up in South Orange, New Jersey. There was no outward show of hatred. But when I look back as a man, I see there was more subtle discrimination. For example, I was a good baseball player. I made the first American Legion team to be formed in South Orange, but they wouldn't issue me a uniform. They used some excuse about my birth certificate.

So I was prepared for the separation at Great Lakes. Back then I went as a tough guy—did a lot of boxing. Some of the guys didn't like me; they thought I was cocky because I was winning all my fights. One of our company leaders made me carry sandbags for five hours before my last fight just to be sure I lost. See, I'd won all my matches within the company, and the next day I was to fight somebody from outside the company for the first time. This guy was an enlisted man and seaman like me. He was black, but he wanted me to lose. But then, so did my own cousin. I had beat him so many times that he was at ringside grinning from ear to ear when I lost. But really I'm glad I lost that fight because the next one would have been with a guy who had been a professional fighter in Philly.

One of the guys who was a boxer later became a shipmate on the *Mason*. Billy Legget became a professional boxer after the service and won eighteen fights in a row. But at Great Lakes he was getting knocked out—so that tells you something about the competition.

Buchanan: We got to Chicago, they shipped us out to the black camp, which was Camp Robert Smalls. No big deal about that.

Graham: I got on the train going to Chicago, to Great Lakes, Illinois. The older guys were smokin' and drinkin' and lyin' and talkin' about women, and we fell right into it—except for the drinkin' and the smokin' and the gamblin'. We arrived in Chicago and went out to Great Lakes. One of the first guys I saw was a guy from my hometown, and he asked if he could borrow five dollars from me. I said, "Sure." He said he'd give it back to me on payday. That was the last time I ever saw him. I have never seen him since.

Garrison: When I went from Columbia, South Carolina, to Great Lakes Naval Training Station, we were in a segregated training camp, Camp Robert Smalls. There were all blacks except that the instructors were white, the officers were white.

Divers: I went down to Prentice Court in Chicago and was sent to Great Lakes, to Camp Robert Smalls. That was the all-black camp. When I went there, it wasn't even completed yet. When they finished building a barracks, they sent another bunch of sailors in to fill it up. We didn't have guns. I went all the way through boot camp without ever seeing a rifle. They just didn't have any at that time. They had one wooden rifle, which we all used for the manual of arms. This was early '42, see.

DuFau: Our country was caught short. There wasn't enough room. They'd already had this camp and changed the name to Robert Smalls. He was a black navy man in the Civil War. A hero. Camp Robert Smalls was across the tracks from the main base. Whenever you had to go to the main base, you had to cross the tracks. When you wanted small stores and stuff like that, you had to go over there. I was in one of the first classes, and being the first was rough. We had to sleep in hammocks: they didn't have sacks; they didn't have the bunks at that time. We were caught short.

Garrison: I don't think any of us ever went over to where the white sailors slept, so we couldn't compare their conditions to ours. We only knew that we were separated. That's my viewpoint; we just knew that we were separated.

DuFau: We never could understand why you had to do so much drilling on that doggone field in Great Lakes. We were supposed to be in the navy. We couldn't understand all of this marching. But it was part of the discipline, developing the discipline habit. You don't ask questions, you follow orders. As I saw it, the navy was making it possible for black men to have rates other than steward's mates and mess attendants. We would be able to have whatever rank we could qualify for. This would be our first opportunity. It wasn't until after the war that I found out this was supposed to be an experiment. At the time, I thought it was just a grand opening. After I found out that it was really an experiment to see if we could do the job, I felt kind of insulted. I'm a human being, and you can trust me like any other human being. I'll get some things; I won't get some others. But when we were at Robert Smalls, we thought we were just part of a program that was opening the way to prove ourselves in a time of war. We had built up a determination among ourselves now that we had this opening. At Robert Smalls we used to try to police each other so that we didn't make a bad record, a bad reputation, because you have bad eggs and good eggs in any group. But we used to sort of police ourselves to see that nobody would make us look bad. After boot camp I went to service school at Great Lakes too. I was in the first class to graduate with rates. That was the winter of '43. I became a signalman third class.

Peters: In order to get into a senior branch of the navy, you had to be a high school graduate. Then they would administer a battery of tests to try to determine what you were best suited for. My test scores indicated that I would be good at radio communications, storekeeper, yeoman, or some paralegal type of job. I chose radio because as a high school kid I was interested in amateur radio, and this kind of fit into my plans. As a matter of fact, I have carried that through because I am an amateur radio operator today.

I went to service school right there in Great Lakes, right at Camp Robert Smalls, for five months. There was constant drilling on the Morse Code and radio theory, typing, and so forth. By the time I graduated, they were only rating 10 percent of each graduating class. There were only eight people in my graduating class, so one person got rated—which wasn't even 10 percent.

I left Great Lakes in November 1943 as a seaman first class radio striker—a striker was somebody who was not rated yet—and my first duty station was in Massachusetts, at an air station just outside of Boston.

Watkins: I went to petty officer school at Robert Smalls, and they told us that the next officers—black officers—were going to come out of that class. It didn't happen. Then they said we were going to get rated, be rated, and *that* didn't happen. So they sent me back to Moffett to train boots. So I trained boots. Then the word came around, "You'd better go to school somewhere, or else you're going to get shipped out." I took the examination, and they said to me, "You can have a choice."

"Can I be in ship's company?"

"Yeah," they said. That meant I could go home every evening. I got something like fourteen dollars extra for eating on the shore. Then they selected the apprentice officers. I was made second platoon leader. I guess I had somebody talking for me because I didn't know anything about platoons and marching. They'd drafted us, and now they had to do something with us.

Buchanan: My scores on the aptitude tests gave me a right to go to service school. They gave you three choices. My first choice was quartermaster. At that time, I thought quartermaster was like with the army, where it's supplies. That didn't bother me. That wouldn't have been a bad job. But it turned out to be navigation, which was way better. Oh, God, I thought that was the greatest thing in the world. I went to quartermaster school, I learned all kinds of signals, and I learned all kinds of navigation. I understood—tried to understand—that thing called radar. You see, it was all new to a lot of people at that time.

Garrison: I took a series of tests to qualify for service school. You see, everybody went through boot camp, but at service school you learned the specialties needed aboard ship. Those who didn't qualify remained seamen—the lowest rank. They sent me to quartermaster school. The quartermaster steers the ship, he plots courses. He's almost like a weather forecaster, and he's the captain's right-hand man.

In service school we had a third-class signalman as our instructor, a big guy. He wanted to show how important ratings were and how outstanding it was for Graham to be second class and DuFau second class and me third class. He told us that competition was so high in the fleet for promotion that in *the entire fleet* they might promote one person to third class, one to second class, and one to first class—in the entire fleet! So when we came in and were able to show that we could qualify for these ratings, it really meant something. Ratings were not easily gotten; you had to work very hard for them. I had some people come aboard the *Mason* as third class, and when they left they were chief petty officers.

You see, third class is the lowest petty officer rating, second class is the next step, then first class, and finally, chief petty officer. A third class petty officer in the navy wears one stripe. If he was in the army, he would have three stripes. When you see a petty officer in the navy with three stripes, it means he's first class. So it's a little different.

One thing I liked about the navy was that almost everyone was a technician. You're prepared to do a specific job, and you must be extremely proficient in that job. There's no room for mediocrity at all. The navy sees to that. They will not rate you unless you're really qualified.

The navy had entrance requirements. We used to say the army would take a warm body, that's all they were interested in. But the navy had high physical standards. You had to be a perfect physical specimen. You had to have high academic attainments. They were really an elite group.

Although the men were making progress within the navy, the same discrimination prevailed in society. In fact, seeing a black man in uniform seemed to incense some—especially if the sleeve of that uniform showed this man had achieved some rank.

DuFau: I don't think I'd ever been a hundred miles away from New Orleans until I went into the service. I'd gone through boot camp, and I got a nine-day leave after the initial training period at Great Lakes. I went home to New Orleans by train, and on my way back to camp, I had to change trains in Atlanta, Georgia. I tried to get a cup of coffee at the lunch counter. I was told there was no coffee, so I told the fellow, "There are two urns going there. That's what I want, coffee."

"We don't *have* any coffee," he said. And then it struck me, what he was really saying to me. I was in uniform and couldn't get a cup of coffee in the train station. It really was like an arrow in me. And I thought, "I'm ready to go into the service to defend *this*?" But that didn't discourage me. It didn't stop me from trying to reach the goal that I was after.

The men found more positive reactions, especially in Chicago, twenty miles from Great Lakes.

Graham: I had sixteen weeks of boot camp, and after that they had examinations to see who would qualify for service school. So I qualified. And I had sixteen weeks of radio school. On the weekends we could go into Chicago. When we got there, the people were so very nice. You'd be walking on the street, and a guy would drive up in his car, with his wife and his daughter, and he would take you to church or take you home and give you dinner. And you know, I can't remember if they were black or white, but we were down on South State Street, which was black. We would go to the Club De Lys and the Carlisle, so it was probably black families. They would take you home, and they would drive you back to Great Lakes from Chicago, which was fantastic.

Garrison: You could go to the theaters free. Those were the days when they had the big bands, and they had fabulous theaters in Chicago.

Graham: And another thing, you could ride the bus and the El free of charge. Yes, the people there in Chicago really treated the servicemen nice.

DuFau: The outstanding memory I have about Chicago was of this annual affair they had called Bud Billiken Day. They had the companies from Great Lakes, Illinois (at that time I was in the third company there), come down and march in the Bud Billiken Day Parade. I have a picture of us parading down the street. I've picked myself out of that long-range shot. I know it's me because that's the way I was positioned, walking in the drill formation.

They treated us with such love. It was just a wonderful, wonderful experience to be the center of attention like that. And we were involved in a *good* thing, a good thing that we were proud of. Pride played a big role in it. A big role.

Dr. Marjorie Joyner: Oh, the people thought they were just wonderful! They *admired them because they admired their uniform* and what they stood for. And the servicemen were just happy to be there. And they felt too that they were doing something to help erase the prejudice line. But you see, it was deeper than any of us thought.

Garrison: What I remember about Chicago was the USO. I think it was the largest USO I've ever seen. They must have had six or more floors. And everything was free: bedding, playing pool, cigarettes, whatever you wanted. That's what I remember. Marva Louis came and Lena Horne came in a few times.

Joyner: Mayor Ed Kelly was very popular at that time. He opened a servicemen's center, but lo and behold, it was for white servicemen, not for black servicemen. Now, you know we weren't going to stand still for *that*. We said, "Well, if you're asking black boys here in Chicago to go abroad and fight for peace, and yet a black boy can't get in a center where there's a white boy and a white girl, we'd better do something to get this thing straightened out."

So Mayor Kelly opened up a servicemen's center on the south side for the black boys and girls, right then and there. That was in Joe Louis's time, and Marva Louis, his wife, was popular with young people. Mayor Kelly had them come as a drawing card. I was a young woman at that time, and he asked me if I would take over Servicemen's Center Number Three, so that we could have a place for black boys and black girls to come to for entertainment after their wartime activity.

And that we did. We'd even go as far as Great Lakes and bring down the sailors from there. The bands and the music made Servicemen's Center Number Three very popular. We had the same activities for the black boys and the black girls that the whites had, but they didn't have to mix. That's where this whole segregation line came back up again. It was the prejudice line, the Mason-Dixon Line that's been in America ever since when. We couldn't move it, but we could be against it. And by being against it, it could be moved one day.

Graham: I remember we were out on Lake Michigan, rowing. We were wearing our peacoats. Some guy was standing on the side watching, and he said, "I smell shit."

"Smell yo' mammy," I said.

Garrison: I know, that was a fight.

Graham: Well, we didn't fight that time, but I was ready for him. Another time we were on the bus going into Chicago with a bunch of white sailors and black sailors. A black girl walked in front of the bus, and a white sailor said, "Boy, if I could catch her, I could put a bag over her head, and I'd go to town," or something to that effect. None of the black sailors said anything. At the next stop, a white girl passed by the bus. I said, "Boy, I wouldn't have to put a bag on her face." We turned the bus out. Things like that. But they always had something derogatory to say.

Garrison: Well, that was the climate then.

Graham: Yes.

Garrison: The whole national feeling was. I'm not saying that about everybody, but most people felt that way.

DuFau: But it was so *built-in*. It was like our national policy. A lot of them felt that's the American way. And you know, we're involved in a conflict—a world war—and we're getting ready to fight for them. But that bitterness just stayed there.

I didn't have much experience of Chicago because by the time I was in service school, my wife had come up from New Orleans with my kid. She was working in Winnetka, Illinois, at a sleep-in job. She and my kid stayed with this family there. So I would leave Great Lakes and go to Winnetka, and then maybe once in awhile we'd ride into Chicago. There were two young boys in the family, maybe about nine or ten, and they tried to teach me how to ice-skate. We went out at five o'clock in the morning to the ice-skating rink because I was ashamed that I couldn't ice-skate. I still don't know how to ice-skate, but those kids tried hard to teach me. But I couldn't get my feet together, and my legs were hurting me so bad because I spread-eagled so much. But my son learned. He'd skate with them, and he did well.

The present commander of Great Lakes Training Center is Adm. Mac Gaston, an African American officer whose first assignment was on a World War II–vintage ship, not that much different from the *Mason*. He is one of the outstanding naval officers whose careers attest to the wider opportunities for blacks in the present U.S. Navy. Nevertheless, Admiral Gaston has faced his share of racial discrimination. For example, his first commander required much more knowledge from him than he did from the white ensigns and assigned him many hours of extra duty if he could not answer obscure questions of naval regulations and lore. Still, Gaston's position as head of the facility that fifty years ago confined black sailors to a separate camp across the tracks speaks for itself.

Adm. Mac Gaston: The navy training center at Great Lakes has conducted training for eighty-two years. Sea readiness *starts* at Great Lakes. It's a process of transition, taking people from civilian life to military life. This is where the impact of training for the fleet starts, right here at Great Lakes.

The technical training that the people who went on the *Mason* received happened right here at Great Lakes. I would not have the opportunity to do what I am doing today had it not been for them paving the way for black people in the navy in a technical way. They were totally successful. They were trained here, and then they went to sea during war and performed their mission.

Not only do you have to learn the technical aspects of things, but you also have to learn how to lead, how to work in a team. It's a great education. And when we talk about education, we're talking about being a good person, being an honest person, having a good heart, and working in team efforts.

Let's take gunner's mate training. First, a recruit goes to boot camp for sixteen weeks. The transition from civilian life to military is not easy. After finishing that boot camp, he would go to an apprentice training, or initial training, called A-school. We still have that kind of training here. Gun school could be as long as twenty weeks or twenty-five weeks. And then he would go to an advanced school, called C-school, to learn more specifically how to repair guns and how to operate them. When a person leaves that gunnery school training and goes to the fleet, all the fear of that gun is removed. He has actually gotten to operate and maintain that equipment in school. So you can take that person on board and go to sea, and he is qualified to shoot that gun and also qualified to repair that gun.

That's true not only in guns but also in electronics, as well as steam, diesel, and gas turbine engineering. And that's the training the *Mason* crew received.

For them to have gone to sea on the *Mason* and completed all the missions and crossings that they did, they had to be qualified, or the ship would have sunk! It would sink right away. That training and that readiness started right here at Great Lakes.

Rated

Classes of trained specialists were graduating from the schools at Camp Robert Smalls week after week—thousands of men. In the navy system, after a man proved his proficiency he was given a rate or rank. First, he was a striker—an apprentice—then third class, second class, first class, and finally chief. Very few—less than 10 percent of every service school class—would leave with a rate, but many of the *Mason* crew did attain their first rates in school. Promotion depended on service, which was mandatory for any real progress. In addition to practical consequences such as an increase in pay, the men wanted the chance to use what they had learned, to test themselves. Plus, they had joined the navy to go to sea. But the navy was still determined to keep these men out of the fleet. The same old arguments were put forth: white sailors could not be asked to live and work with black sailors aboard ship; black sailors would not respond well under fire; a modern warship with all its sophisticated equipment could not be risked, etc. So the men found themselves at shore stations or on small coastal vessels.

But even when duty was on shore, the navy placed restrictions on the black sailors. For example, as the Bureau of Naval Personnel report (which summarized the navy's "research" on its African American members) states, "Careful instructions were given to Negro shore patrols that they make no effort to discipline whites and that even in a case of a fight between men of different races, they restrict themselves to handling the colored participants" (36). Again, white "sensibilities" were pandered to, and even a simple change such as creating a rating for steward's mates "in order to give honor to men who had served long and well" resulted in a flood of protests that saw this "as a willful insult to the men who had already been proudly wearing the eagle" (36).

If white sailors were incensed at just seeing a black man with a rating badge on his uniform, even a member of the steward's branch, how, the navy wondered, would they react to black men qualified to wear the top petty officer's ratings—radioman, quartermaster, radar man, chief? "One strong argument made for holding Negroes to a narrow range of billets was that otherwise the races would have to be mingled and the problem of Negro petty officers exercising command over white seamen would present itself" (35).

Reading such statements now brings the images of Gen. Colin Powell, Adm. Mac Gaston, Capt. Gene Kendall, and tens of thousands of outstanding African American officers and servicemen and women to mind. These men and women represent the most powerful arguments against the words of the report and the assumptions that underlie them. Perhaps in the years to come the discriminating attitudes of the present will appear just as benighted and, it is hoped, antiquated. But in 1943, "so firm was the assumption that they would not serve in the fleet that the matter was scarcely discussed" (40).

Buchanan: I came out of service school and was sent down to Cape May, New Jersey. I realized that the black sailors were being used to relieve white sailors so they could go out to the fleet. They needed them so bad. Then I heard that things were going to happen, that we might get more than shore duty.

They put me on a patrol boat. We were going out on a regular basis, out on the coast of New Jersey. Our ship was just an eighty-foot yacht, painted all gray. All that beautiful teak wood on the yacht painted gray. It looked just awful. But the ship was nice, and it was a small crew, about eleven people. We had only a couple of officers. We'd go out off the coast and patrol, sweeping the whole harbor.

One night I was on the fantail, down at the stern of the ship. I said to the officer (I was steering the ship), "What happens if we do see a submarine?"

He says, "We ram. We set the depth charges at thirty feet and we ram."

"And where are we going to be when we ram with this little piece of wood against a submarine?"

"We'll be in the water."

"When those depth charges go off, where are we going to be?"

"We have to figure that out."

"Oh, man!" I groaned. I didn't know what this patrolling was all about. That seemed a little odd.

Graham: After finishing boot training and class-A radioman school at Camp Robert Smalls, Great Lakes, five shipmates and I were transferred to Cape May Naval Air Base in Cape May, New Jersey. I was a petty officer third class, but I was doing seaman work on the piers. I learned a lot about seamanship from a shipmate in charge. I do not remember his rank. (He was a white shipmate from Georgia.)

I was discouraged and disappointed that I was not assigned to a ship. I longed to go aboard a ship and sail the "Ocean Blue." My chance came at last. I was transferred to a minesweeper (the *Blue Jay*). This minesweeper was no more than a fishing boat, or trawler, converted to a minesweeper.

The first day out I got so seasick that I was unable to do any work. I remember praying to the Lord that if I ever returned to shore, I would never go to sea again. You know what? I was back on this minesweeper and out to sea the next day. I never did get seasick again.

Though the men were moving into positions of responsibility, the old problems of discrimination continued. Even in a northern state like New Jersey, in a town like Cape May, whose economy at this time depended on its naval base, there was prejudice against the black sailors.

Divers: I was shipped out to the Philadelphia Navy Yard. In Philly, I was put in charge of a draft—that's a group of sailors being sent from one base to another—to Cape May, New Jersey, for assignment at Cape May at the naval section base and air base.

We arrived in Cape May with meal tickets. I had asked the guy who'd given them to me, "Are there any special places that this meal ticket is good for?"

He said, "This meal ticket is a United States Government meal ticket; it's as good as the money in your pocket."

"Fine, that's good," I said. So we got off the train, and we were all hungry. I was in charge of the draft. We went into this one restaurant. Everybody was seated. The lady came out from behind the counter, and she looked at us, and she ran back to the rear of the restaurant. After awhile, another lady came up, and she said, "What can I do for you?"

"Well, we've got our meal tickets here, and we want to be served."

She said, "Oh, no. No. No, no, not here, not here."

"What's the problem?" I asked. "Are you running out of food? Are you fixin' to close up?"

"No. We don't serve you . . . you people here."

"What? In New Jersey?"

"Yes, sir. I'm sorry."

"Well," I said, "I can't figure this out. Here we are in New Jersey. I expect it in certain parts of the South, but not up here."

In the meantime, people had gathered outside the restaurant and were peeping in the window. It attracted the attention of the shore patrol. The shore patrol comes in and says, "What's the problem?" So I told them. They said, "Don't worry about that. We'll get you something to eat. Come on out, come on out. You guys come on out and line up here. I got transportation coming for you." Anyway, here comes a big navy van, a big dray, what we call eighteen-wheelers now. And we all climbed aboard and went right to the United States Navy Mess Hall, where we finally got served, in our own facility. They would not honor our meal ticket there in New Jersey. I couldn't believe it.

I was more surprised than I was angry, because to me, at my age, at that time, it was just a new experience.

Graham: While stationed at Cape May Naval Air Station, I remember several fights with white sailors in the mess hall. One day I went to the first chow call and returned to the barracks. Someone yelled, "There's a fight going on in the mess hall between white and colored sailors." Several of us ran back to the mess hall to discover cups and food trays flying in all directions!

But another time, in Wildwood, New Jersey, a few miles from Cape May, several shipmates and I went to the one and only theater. We sat downstairs in the center section. No sooner did we sit down than the usher came over and informed us that we could not sit where we were and directed us to the "colored" section. We refused. He went to get the manager. While he was gone, the four or five white sailors sitting behind us asked us not to move and stated that they were with us. The manager never did approach us. The next time we attended that movie theater, all sailors sat in the same designated area.

The new technology that was coming to the navy presented opportunities, but each step forward came at a price.

Gordon: When I finished boot camp they gave us our general classifications and our scores. My tests were high enough for me to become a quartermaster. They sent me to the outgoing unit for transportation to quartermaster school. But while I was waiting for transportation to that school, they came down one day and told us we were going to take another test. There were about five or six of us. We didn't know what it was all about; it was just another test, and they had given us so many. They gave us this series of sounds. They would give us five sounds, and we were to pick which sound didn't belong among the five. Some of the sounds would be ascending notes, some of them would be descending notes, and some would just be steady notes. One would be different.

As a result of this test, they decided who would become sonar men. At that time, the navy didn't have any such rate as sonar man. They had what they called soundmen, which was not a special rating; it was just a job function. This was a new technology: equipment with which they would detect submarines.

We were sent to Cape May, New Jersey, to the Admiral Hotel, which was made a navy facility because of the war. They had set up a school there primarily for black enlisted men. They didn't want us going to the schools in the South and to be integrated with the white navy enlisted men. I was in the first school of sonar men and was one of the navy's first sonar operators.

When we graduated from Cape May, New Jersey, we were all promoted to petty officer third class. But there was a quandary. They didn't have a rating badge for sonar men because it was a brand-new rate. The top four rates in the navy were worn on the right arm; the rest of the rating badges in the navy were worn on the left arm. Quartermaster was probably the top-ranking rate category, and so they gave us a quartermaster rate to wear on our left arm! That caused some concern. Here's this group of black guys walking down the street with a quartermaster rate backwards on their left arm. We took some ridicule for that, but that didn't last long because they soon came out with the sonar rating badge.

DuFau: I was in the draft that came to New York City. I was so lucky, because I had an aunt who lived in New York City. The name beneath mine went to California. I was just lucky by one name, because all those guys in my class that went to California were killed in this big explosion at Port Chicago when they were loading ammunition.* One name and I would have been dead! I didn't know that then. All I knew was that I had a foothold to reach New York, to see the big city. I got off the train, onto a truck with all my baggage, and we went out to Pier 6, Staten Island, then off the truck onto what they call a picket boat. I had never been on any navy vessel like that.

Right from the pier we took off. There used to be a submarine net spread, and we went beyond that. They opened the net and let us out. I was so frightened. We all were. I was wondering whether we were trying to catch up with some ship that had left the harbor because I wasn't prepared for all that fast movement. But they brought us outside the harbor to the *Ambrose*. It was a light ship out there. And there was an examination vessel called the USS *Speyer Allen*. It was the examination vessel for New York harbor. And I spent ten months out there.

Roberts: I went to Hampton Institute in Virginia to be trained as an electrician's mate. We had to learn a lot of math—trigonometry and algebra. But it come easy to me. School has always been easy for me. I could listen in class and then pass the exam. I enjoyed the electrical math. Then I went to Norfolk. My cousin who'd gone into the navy with me was there too, and we had our own private room. We'd gone all through boot camp together—swung our hammocks side by side. Here we were in Norfolk in this private room at the end of the barracks. See, the other men in the barracks were in the stewards branch, so this was how they separated us.

Well, there I was, trained as an electrician, but the job they gave me was pushing airplanes around on the airfield. I did that

---

* For the story of the tragic loss of 202 black sailors and the unjust treatment of the survivors see *The Port Chicago Mutiny* by Robert L. Allen (Warner Books, 1989).

for quite a while. But one day they had this southern chief petty officer out there seeing that everyone worked hard. We were loading scrap iron and he was calling out "Heave-ho, Heave-ho" like we were working on the railroad or on a chain gang. I said, "Look, Buddy, I'm not pushing any more airplanes. Give me a job doing the work I was trained for. I'll work my tail off."

He looked at me. He was shocked. He said, "I'm going to send you up to see the head chief petty officer."

"I don't care. Send me up to President Roosevelt. It still stands. I'm not pushing airplanes."

I went up to see the chief. I never will forget him. He was an old guy with hash marks all the way up to his neck. He had been told I was a problem, but he just said, "Have a seat." I sat down. He said, "They tell me you don't want to push airplanes around anymore."

"You got that right," I replied.

"What kind of work did you do before you went into the service?" he asked.

"I worked for the federal government in the war department, in the Pentagon building. I started out working in the mailroom, and from there I went into specifications, which was a good job. There were only three people in my department."

"Ever do any filing?" he asked.

"We did a little in specification," I told him.

"Think you can handle it?"

"Sure," I answered. He sent me around to a warrant officer who had a little anteroom with a desk near his office. The warrant officer told me that this would be my desk and that I would process invoices for airplane parts. I had to make out invoices only two or three times a day and file a few pieces of paper. The rest of the time I listened to the radio and slept. I figured, though, that if that's what they wanted me to do, that's what I would do.

Garrison: When I graduated from service school I was assigned to East Boston Section Base—that's in Boston. I was on a small wooden ship called the *A-48*, which had a wooden hull and deck. We went out every night, out of the harbor, and we dropped hydrophones over the side into the water, put earphones on, and listened for submarines, if any were coming. And in the morning we went back to the base.

I did that for about three months, and then I was assigned to a minesweeper, the *Puffin* (AMC-29). We swept mines from Boston, up to Maine, and back. I used to see the ships coming into Boston harbor and the guys standing at parade, and I wanted to get aboard one of those larger ships. I actually requested sea duty. I decided to try to be promoted to signalman. On the *Puffin* they had a third-class signalman, but he couldn't do the job. We had to challenge every vessel that approached, and he just couldn't take the messages. So the chief would tell me to do it. Though I was a seaman first class, I had taken a series of tests to be promoted to signalman, because they didn't need quartermasters. And the day before I would have taken the final test, they called down and told me to pack my bags, I was going to Norfolk. I told the chief, "Chief, I'm supposed to take my test."

"Sorry," he said, "you have to go."

Divers: I was assigned to a minesweeper. They needed a quartermaster, so I worked on the USS *Flamingo*, which was very good duty at that time because it was what we call a nine-to-five job. We'd leave early in the morning, go out five fathoms, sweep the channel, and turn around and come back. That was our duty, six days a week; we even got a day off. That was considered *good* duty. Some of us even slept on the base; you didn't have to sleep aboard the ship.

Then I was assigned to the Office of Navigational Information, which was the hydrographic office on the base. I stayed there until another slot came up for a quartermaster on another minesweeper, the *Blue Jay*. I sailed aboard the *Blue Jay*, and then I was transferred back to the highly secret duty concerned with code breaking. I worked in the office where they invented codes. We had classified information that had to be sent out to different locations throughout the North Atlantic in the theater of war.

Buchanan: On patrol duty we used to find fresh bread wrappings right off the coast, and we always thought the fishermen were taking bread out to the submarines. It might have been true. I have no way of knowing because, see, I don't know whether the records show that a submarine came in and got resupplied. But that was one of the things that submarines were doing all up and down the coast. They had places to go in and get supplies, whatever they needed.

Anyway, we paid attention. Anything we saw with a light on it, we chased. We'd catch up to it and tell them, "Turn those lights out," something like that, with a bullhorn.

Living on the yacht was nice. One night I got sick. I had been in town, Cape May, and had had a lot to drink. I got aboard the ship and went right down to the galley and pulled out a Boston cream pie. I ate the *whole* thing and promptly threw up over the side. I never did that again, you can believe it.

Now, I was perfectly happy down there, doing the patrols. Eventually, I wound up on the signal tower. We had a thing called flag hoists. When the ships were in a line, you'd throw the flag hoist up. Each ship copies the leader's flag hoist. You'd wait awhile and then strike it down. Every ship makes the exact move. I liked how everybody moved when I pulled the flag!

Once a ship came into the coast in a fog. He didn't know where he was, but he knew the coast was in front of him. He started to signal. Now, I was on the signal bridge by myself. (This story tells why I got selected to go on the *Mason*.) I answered him, and he gave me the signal. I called it into the base. Later on, I found out it was something very important. I don't know what it was. I got the message through and that was important.

As more and more of the qualified black sailors graduating from Great Lakes demonstrated their ability in shore stations, pressure built on the navy. Why train these men and then forbid them to serve on a warship? the black community asked. But just as with the earlier decision to activate black recruits, change came more in response to white concerns than black demands for just treatment. The Bureau of Naval Personnel report states: "[H]eightened problems of morale and tension were created by large concentrations of Negro personnel in shore activities, by white sentiments that Negroes were not sharing the fighting, and by Negro resentment against being barred from the fighting" (41).

In addition, reports were coming back from commanders who had black sailors working with them. The following was written by a commanding officer on Staten Island, where Lorenzo DuFau served: "Some of our patrol craft are almost entirely manned by them, and the duties they have performed during an unusually severe winter have been arduous, hazardous, and under conditions of temperature anything but comfortable. They are serving on tugs, in running boats, minesweepers (this last is an experimental effort), on deck and in engine rooms, and the measure of service has been of a uniformly high standard. There has been, by my order, no coddling, and they have met the test" (46).

As more and more black sailors "met the test," and in view of "white sentiments" and "Negro resentment," the navy decided to allow black sailors to man warships. One DE, the USS *Mason,* and one PC "would be manned so far as possible, by enlisted Negroes under white officers; all enlisted billets would be filled by Negroes as soon as men qualified to fill them had been trained" (42).

Rumors started to circulate about a ship that wanted black sailors. The navy began to look among its black enlisted personnel for men to make up the crew of a destroyer escort, the USS *Mason.*

Graham: I had never heard of a DE before. I thought they were looking for men to go on a destroyer. I was ready. There were two of us on the base trained as radiomen: my friend Patterson was second class, and I was a third-class petty officer. They wanted a second-class petty officer, but Patterson was deathly afraid of the water, so I jumped for the opportunity. But the chief said, "You're only third class; we wanted second class." So the communications officer told the chief to give me the radio manual for me to study. At a certain time he'd call me in and give me the exam, and if I qualified, I could go aboard. Patterson helped me study. I went in, took the exam, and passed. On December 15, 1943, he called me in; I had passed. He said, "Well, you can go aboard ship." They didn't say it was an experimental ship or anything. They said it was a DD, which means a destroyer. So I jumped for joy. At last I was going on board a ship.

I think one reason, more or less, why I got transferred to the *Mason* was because they had navy women, the WAVES (Women Accepted for Voluntary Emergency Service), coming in. They had this big radio shack, and the white WAVES—they didn't have black WAVES until October 1944—came to work in the radio shack. All the white guys would stand there and look, and I would do the same thing. There was an old chief there. My gosh, he would turn red every time I looked at them. They came through the door, and I came up to see them with everybody else. And he didn't like it.

Buchanan: There was another black sailor on duty with me. We used to swim in the ocean all the time. We had these dumb ideas that we'd swim out to the porpoises and things. We would try, but we never could get to the porpoises. We were *good* friends, but I got selected over him to go on the *Mason.*

At this particular time my brother (actually he's my brother-in-law, but I think of him as my brother) had come down to me and he said he was leaving—he was going on this destroyer. Now, the story was getting around that they were going to make this destroyer with a black crew. It was only a destroyer escort, really no comparison with a real destroyer. I wanted a destroyer, not a destroyer escort. I knew the difference. My brother-in-law-to-be was bragging about the fact that he owed me six dollars. Now, in World War II, if somebody owed you six dollars, that was *a lot of money.* And I said, "No, no, you're not going nowhere without me. I want my six dollars." We argued about this thing for days. Then, finally, the officers came down and told me, "Do you know you got selected to go on the destroyer?"

"What?" I cried. I ran up to the base. (At this time I was living aboard a ship.) I ran up to the base and I told Graham, and that just tickled him to death. That was fun. We had been together so long, right from Chicago and Great Lakes, and he was happy that we were going together. But he wasn't getting away with the six dollars. That was *in my mind,* you understand?

But we got shipped out from there down to Norfolk to go to school for the *Mason.*

At Norfolk the crew attended classes aimed at equipping them for life on a destroyer escort at sea. These included abandon-ship and fire drills, as well as further training in each man's specialty. Their skipper, Capt. William Blackford, visited Norfolk and interceded for the crew when problems arose.

Graham: On December 18, 1943, I was transferred and received at the naval station in Norfolk, Virginia. I learned, right away, the reason why the place was called "Shit City." Every other day there was an incident with white and "Negro" sailors. The white sailors and the base commander thought that we should be treated the same as the steward's mates. No reflection on the steward's mates, but we were enlisted in the seaman branch of the United States Navy, same as the whites, and we demanded the respect. Captain Blackford came to our aid, incident after incident.

At the theater we were directed to use the rear entrance with the steward's mates. We refused. Captain Blackford, again, came to our rescue. Rules changed. All enlisted personnel—black and white alike—used the same designated entrance area. Commissioned officers used the main entrance.

Jane Blackford (letter to her parents): Bill stayed with the Crenshaws in Norfolk but had little chance to see much of them as he was in conference with captains and admirals, etc., most of one day and looking over his crew and working with the Exec. the rest of the time. About that crew—it isn't quite as mixed as we thought. It's all colored except some of the chief petty officers and officers. They are all handpicked and have all had some sea experience. Bill is much luckier, as far as that goes, than some of the other skippers.

As the navy report states, originally, the *Mason* crew was to "represent a cross section of the Navy's Negroes" (42). Again, the thinking seemed based on a view of "the Navy's Negroes" as some kind of monolithic group, a "new and strange problem." But the voice of common sense reasserted itself, and the bureau decided to choose the crew for the *Mason* "on the premise that all commanding officers deserve the best crews that can be furnished, whether Negro or white" (42). Therefore, though the sailors were not selected by name, the orders that went out stated that the best men should be picked by the officers on the spot.

Divers: I had been called over to personnel one day and was told that I was going to be transferred. I said, "Transferred to where?"

The fellow replied, "The USS *Mason*."

I said, "What kind of ship is that?"

He said, "Well, you know as much about it as we do." So they sent us to Norfolk, Virginia, and Portsmouth for precommissioning school.

I had had no experience with segregation so I wasn't used to the way things were in Norfolk. Coming back from liberty one night, a bunch of marines and sailors and I were waiting on the trolley. When the trolley came up, we all climbed aboard, and the trolley just sat there. So the guys all hollered, "Hey, Mac, let's get this thing going. We've got to get back to the base."

"I can't move this trolley until this fellow gets to the rear," the driver said.

"Get to the rear? What do you mean?"

And he said, "Oh, all the Negroes have got to go to the rear."

So they said, "How is he going to get to the rear?"

"Well, he'll have to get off then."

So I said, "Well, what the heck is this?" But I didn't want to make it tough on the rest of the guys, so I said I would get off and catch the next trolley—I would be first in line and could get to the rear.

But those guys said, "No way, Mac. You stay right aboard."

Then they took the tiller away from that guy on the trolley and threw the conductor off. They took that thing all the way— nonstop—all the way down to the base. And we didn't have no problems with those guys after that—to my knowledge.

Gordon: I was on liberty in Norfolk with three other sailors from the *Mason,* and, of course, I stood out for obvious reasons. I remember a car pulling up that was loaded with people, and somebody yelled and cussed me out because I was a nigger lover and was with those black sailors. And we just took it in stride and laughed it off and kept on going. But that was a constant type of harassment.

Garrison: So I went down to Norfolk. When I got down there they didn't need signalmen or quartermasters, but they were short of radiomen. But you had to learn how to type, and you had to learn the Morse code by sound—I knew it by sight. So I went to the base library and got a book to teach me how to touch-type, and I learned. I studied how to place my fingers and practiced on my own. At that time the navy didn't have time to train people in some skills; you just had to know. Then I took the test for radioman, and I became a radioman third class. So I was sure, then, to be assigned to the *Mason.*

DuFau: When they made up the draft for the *Mason,* that's when I was taken from the light ship and sent to service school. At Norfolk I was exposed to some things that just weren't so pleasant. For a couple of days we had to eat with the steward's mates. We weren't in the regular barracks like the others at the school. We were in a Quonset hut setup.

Buchanan: We never should have been put in those so-called barracks at Norfolk. Now, I had to have a shower *every* day. I didn't miss. In fact, when I was in boot camp, I didn't miss a shower any day. If there was a guy that *wouldn't* shower, we took a scrub brush and scrubbed his butt down, and he stayed clean for the rest of the time he was around us. Everybody kept themselves very clean. I remember one time when I walked in the snow out to the shower, with practically no clothes on, and took a shower in *cold* water. That's how bad this barracks was. They were Quonset huts.

I went to sleep that night and I couldn't move in the morning. My brother-in-law was a couple of bunks over. We were supposed to go out on a ship on training that day. I said to him, "I can't move." So they left without me to go to the ship. They left me there to go to the sick bay. I went to the sick bay, and they acted like I was faking it! I was so sick by the time the afternoon came that they wound up putting me in a hospital. I spent thirty days in the hospital with scarlet fever. That's what I caught that night, scarlet fever, in those barracks. I'll never forgive the navy for that.

Thirty days. And they let me out in thirty days only because I *begged* the doctors, "I don't want to miss my ship." They were very nice to me. I never had to do any work in there. I slept next to a guy who had been in the Mediterranean, who was there because his eardrums were busted from the bombardment that he went through on a destroyer. I thought about all this stuff that I was getting into.

But I said to myself, "Well, I'm going to go to war, I'm going to get killed." The nicest thing about the navy is you can't drink all that water, but you ain't coming home with no legs. You understand? That was always in the back of my head. I wasn't going to eat no mud, I wasn't going to have that problem. I was going to live pretty clean—no big deal. Which is what happened to me. I lived very clean in the navy, and I ate every day. Even if it was during a storm, if you put some food in front of me, I ate.

Graham: Late one night in Norfolk, when several shipmates returning from liberty approached the main gate, the marine on duty demanded that we remove the chevron from our sleeves and enter the base from another gate reserved for steward's mates. We had a few choice words with him, still walking fast, yelling back and forth. Suddenly, we heard the cocking of his carbine. Boy! Did we take off!

Reports of such incidents caused the navy's personnel bureau report to finally observe, "One of the strongest complaints of the Negroes is his resentment at not having the chance to use his competence on its own merits" (65). The indignities suffered by the *Mason* crew while in Norfolk came while (as the navy report admits) "High morale and superior grades marked the men's performance throughout their special DE training" (66).

At Norfolk they attended school with white sailors, competed and succeeded, yet a marine guard could still order a man to remove his hard-earned ratings badge, or the usher at a movie theater could insist that an American serviceman come in through the back door.

Roberts: I had a very bad experience at Norfolk. It was Thanksgiving Day. I went to the chow hall, and the chaplain was holding a service out on the lawn. It was a bright sunny day, and I really felt thankful to the Lord that I was in Norfolk on a bright sunny day when there were other sailors and soldiers overseas dying at that very moment. I had very deep feelings inside. Thankful for my own safety and praying for them and for peace. I left the parade grounds and went into the chow hall for Thanksgiving dinner. Now in Norfolk, we were segregated: black sailors sat in the back of the chow hall. So I went where I sat every day. A little young white sailor came up to me and said, "Move farther back."

I said, "No, I'm not moving, buddy."

"Well, I'll report you."

"I don't give a damn who you report. I'm not moving one inch."

He left, saying he was going to go to the base commander. I sat there thinking. I hadn't eaten any Thanksgiving dinner. I just sat there. Then I remembered there was a gun on the file cabinet in the office of the warrant officer I worked for. It was there every day. I jumped up and raced back there. I couldn't see anything but red. It was as if somebody threw a red blanket over my head. Everything was red. I tore that office up looking for that gun. It wasn't where it usually was. If I had found that gun I would have shot every white person that came into view. I'm not that hateful; I had just lost it, that's all. I went out and sat behind a hangar. I was more or less in a daze. I just sat there for ten or fifteen minutes. Then the cloud was lifted; that red blanket just disappeared. I felt very calm, and that was the end of that. I often think when I hear of people getting in trouble through sudden outbursts of temper, "Gee, that could have been me!" If that gun had been there, my whole life would have changed.

Garrison: The *Mason* was an experiment. They wanted to see if we could take to the sea. They wanted to see if we were capable of becoming regular sailors and fitting in with the white guys. But they were going to keep us segregated and separated for as long as they possibly could because the navy was the last stronghold. They did not want us there. They didn't want any part of us, and they didn't know what to do with us.

DuFau: Our guys had gone to service school. When you finished service school you would come out maybe seaman third class or maybe first or second, or you might strike for a whole year. You might be a radioman striker. That meant you would apply yourself for a length of time before you got a stripe. When we went aboard ship, about 90 percent of the guys had been to service school. There were some strikers that waited to get a rating, but many of us were rated when we went aboard. The idea was that we would move up in ratings until we had relieved any of the white petty officers ahead of us. And by the end we had. We had quite a few chief petty officers, and by the very end we had two black officers.

Peters: I heard about the *Mason* because a friend of mine who had preceded me at Great Lakes was a gunner's mate who had been sent out to Vallejo, California. Through correspondence with him I found out that the *Mason* was going to be an actuality. I volunteered for it because I wanted to be a part of the seagoing navy as opposed to being land based. There were some black navy enlisted people, most of them rated, I guess, who were serving on small ships like minesweepers. Some were on the coastal patrol, and some were on yard tugs. But I really wanted a warship. That's what I was looking for.

I figured if I was going to have to participate in the war, I should be in the thick of it, as opposed to sitting it out on some shore station. I applied for a program for naval aviators. I was at an air station. There were two slots, and the two people who came out tops on the exam were to be selected to go down to Pensacola, Florida, and become naval aviators. Four of us took the exam—two black, two white. The two black fellows, myself and Dan Motley, came out on top on the exam. Then they changed the selection process. "We're going to make our selections based on the length of time that you've been in the navy." Motley and I had been in the navy only a little over a year. These other two fellows had been in a couple of more months. So they were the ones who were selected for V-12 and went down to Pensacola and became aviators, and Motley and I went aboard the *Mason*.

This was a constant kind of thing you saw going on in the navy. Anytime you achieved—or thought you had achieved—something, the rules would be changed, and that achievement would be thrown out. This was pretty much indicative of the way that the *Mason*'s history would be handled. You read about all of these other ships, but even though we always came out number one in all of our exercises and inspections, you don't hear anything about the *Mason*.

Commissioning and Shakedown

On October 14, 1943, when the keel of the USS *Mason* was laid, the U-boats were a formidable adversary. The Germans had sunk eleven merchant vessels in the North Atlantic that month alone. The *Mason* was launched on November 17, 1943 and commissioned on March 20, 1944. She was sponsored by Mrs. David N. Mason in honor of her son Ens. Newton Henry Mason. Ensign Mason enlisted in the Naval Reserve in 1940. At age twenty-one he became a naval aviator and piloted a fighter plane in the Pacific. He was shot down by Japanese aircraft in aerial combat during the Battle of the Coral Sea on May 8, 1942. Ensign Mason received the Distinguished Flying Cross. Most DEs were named for young men killed in battle, and the navy chose this *Evert*-class DE to carry Ensign Mason's name. There had been an earlier *Mason* named for a former Secretary of the Navy, an ancestor of Ensign Mason's. When Mrs. Mason broke the bottle of champagne over the ship, no one knew that the *Mason* would play a historic role. David Mason, Newton Mason's nephew, remembers how proud his grandparents were of the ship named for their son. "It was spoken of often," he recalls, "but it was only after I met Jim Graham that I realized how special the crew was."

All the crews of destroyer escorts were unique in that they were trained for the specifics of antisubmarine warfare, which included learning to keep constantly alert in spite of the tedium of long slow days at sea. But only the *Mason* would have the distinction of being the one U.S. warship taken into combat by a predominately black crew. A smaller antisubmarine vessel, the *PC-1264* (a submarine chaser), would have a crew of fifty-two black sailors, nine enlisted men, and white officers. She patrolled coastal waters around the United States and the Caribbean. The first black U.S. Navy admiral,

Samuel Gravely, served on the *PC-1264*. But only the *Mason* would cross the ocean eight times, escort convoys, take on the U-boats, and carry her 160 black crewmen into history. Her captain, William Blackford, had been assigned to the ship before it was decided that the *Mason* would have a black crew. The same voices that had urged the navy to open its ranks now asked what was happening to all these well-trained sailors.

The *Mason* was the navy's answer: a way to meet two demands with one ship. After the fall of France left Britain isolated, its survival depended on the merchant ships and the huge oil tankers that brought food, medicine, clothing, and fuel—as well as weapons and ammunition—from North America. But hundreds of German U-boats were sinking these ships with impunity. Even after the United States entered the war the successful assault continued. The troop ships became even more enticing targets. By April 1942 the Allies had lost one million tons of cargo, and by December the German submarines had sunk 1,161 merchant vessels. More than forty thousand lives would be lost at sea. Though destruction at Pearl Harbor was more dramatic, the loss of life and material during the early phases of the Battle of the Atlantic represented a more serious threat. The U-boats had to be stopped or the Nazis would win the war.

The navy developed the destroyer escort to combat the German submarines and to protect the convoy. Smaller than a destroyer, less expensive and yet capable of high speeds (twenty to twenty-four knots), the DE had substantial weapons designed for submarine combat. These included depth charges—fifty-gallon drums stuffed with up to six hundred pounds of explosives—and "hedgehogs"—a charge consisting of twenty-four projectiles fired ahead of the ship that scatters shot over a wide area. In addition, the ship carried armaments on her decks: mounted 3-inch, .50-caliber guns and smaller antiaircraft guns that were easy to maneuver.

The most revolutionary aspect of the DE was its sophisticated tracking systems, which used high-frequency radios, radar, and sonar equipment. Scientists at the Princeton Institute such as Albert Einstein had joined the war effort and found ways to use sound beams to locate submarines. The sonar operator sent out the beam and then analyzed the reflected sound wave. The U-boats could no longer sneak into the convoys as they had done, nor could they submerge undetected. Radar supplemented the twenty-four-hour watch the sailors maintained. Radiomen could intercept even the most fleeting communication between subs. These escort vessels cost about five million dollars each, and in the fall of 1942, President Roosevelt made building them a top priority. Eventually, 565 DEs went into service and helped win the Battle of the Atlantic.

George Polk, a petty officer on the *Mason*, told this story in a speech he made in 1981. He died years before this project began, but he was so devoted to the ship, it seems only right to include him.

George Polk: Lt. Comdr. William M. Blackford, USNR, was the first skipper of the USS *Mason*. From time to time he was subjected to sarcastic remarks from the other ship captains relative to the fact that his crew, for the most part, was black. The following is a true excerpt from one such conversation, as recorded by a war correspondent.

"Blackford, you must have somewhat of a problem with all those niggers on your ship, and so few white men," the captain of another ship said to him.

Almost angrily Captain Blackford responded, "Contrary to what you want to believe, I have less of a problem than you. We get along fine and do our jobs with no trouble of any sort. I regard my ship to be just like any of the hundreds of DEs on the high seas, not as a problem child nor as an experiment. I am not a crusader, and I am not trying to solve the race problem. I am simply trying to run a good navy fighting ship. Actually, my men get into less trouble than those from other ships because they know how to behave."

At this point I would like to say for "Big Bill," as we among ourselves affectionately called him (and I wish he were present to hear me say this), as a crew, to a man, we would have probably followed him to hell and back.

DuFau: Our first captain, William Blackford, was a captain indeed, and a man I will always have love and respect for. From the very beginning he was straight with us. He used to meet with the leading petty officers aboard ship. We would meet in the wardroom. There were few times you ever had a chance to be in the wardroom. That was like no man's land, except for those gold braids. But he used to call the leading petty officers from each division and sit and talk with us. This was just between him and his crew. He wanted to know if there were any problems on the ship that he should know about or that he could sort of work out. Because he didn't want any conflict on the ship.

And he advised us that, "As long as you do your job, what your rank calls for, you'll have no problem. I am just here to run a U.S. Navy ship. I am not here to solve a race problem." He said, "As long as you carry out your navy duties, you are going to get along with me. But if you cross lines, I am going to come down on you." And he meant that. He lived up to it. He was a living example of it.

I will always have respect for that man, because he developed a thinking among the men. He was part of making life aboard ship so wonderful. We used to call him—not to his face—"Big Bill."

Capt. William Blackford (letter to his parents): Boston, Mass. 9 January 1944: The ship is coming along fine but they put commissioning day back to 16 Feb. Am sure we will have a good crew as have some very fine reports concerning them. Can't figure out why I was picked but will do the best I can—really quite an opportunity to do something.

William Blackford was never sure why he had been selected for this command. He had been named captain before it was decided that the ship would be manned with black sailors. Perhaps only chance was responsible, but if so, it was a happy chance. In every discussion of their captain each crew member used the same phrase, "We would have followed him to hell and back." William Blackford was born in Seattle, Washington. His father, a doctor who had founded one of Seattle's first hospitals, was a dedicated sailor. William Blackford grew up on the family's yacht, the *Sally Bruce*, learning the seamanship that would earn him the respect and grati-tude of his crew. Before his assignment to the *Mason* he spent a year and a half commanding the USS *Phoebe*, a minesweeper operating in the Aleutian Islands. Blackford had been a Naval Reserve midship-man at the University of Washington during his undergraduate work there. He had then gone on to study at the University of Virginia and was two semesters shy of a Ph.D. in chemistry when he went on active duty in January 1941.

The Blackford family had originally come from Virginia; in fact, the Blackfords were prominent in the state's history as educators and physicians. Though the navy's personnel department did not know this, Blackford's great-grandmother, Mary Berkeley Minor Blackford (1802–1896), was a celebrated abolitionist. Her story is told in *Mine Eyes Have Seen the Glory* (Harvard University Press, 1951), subtitled the "Story of a Virginia Lady Who Taught Her Sons to Hate Slavery and to Love the Union." The author, Dr. L. Minor Blackford, a cousin of William Blackford's described "the forcefulness displayed by Mary Blackford in her relentless fight against slavery." Quoted in the book are the writings of Mrs. Blackford, including this passage:

> I only know of one insurrection before this of Nat Turner's, and of none since. And I am sure that with an hundredth part of the wrongs they suffer we white people would have risen in arms fifty times.

> How the practice of injustice hardens the feelings is perfectly wonderful; what is done under our own eyes would shock us to the last degree were it not for this hardening process. I am convinced that the time will come when we shall look back and wonder how Christians could sanction slavery.

> I have been this morning to witness the departure in the Steam boat from this place to Norfolk on their way to Liberia of one hundred and eight liberated slaves. . . . Thus opening a way, I humbly trust, for great good to Africa and to this country.

Mine Eyes Have Seen the Glory also contains copies of the letters the slaves freed by the Blackford family wrote back to them from Liberia, in which they keep Mrs. Blackford informed of their progress and urge her to "tell all who want to come, come." Still, the sons of Mary Berkeley Minor Blackford served in the Confederate Army during the Civil War. Charles Blackford wrote to his mother in 1853: "I admit the full force of all you say of the evils of slavery: But would my going North cause these evils to recur less frequently? The same reasons which you apply to me should make all holding my opinions leave the South,—and suppose they did! Who would there then be to regulate public opinion? Who to prevent even more flagrant acts of injustice and cruelty? Who to lighten their yoke? You certainly would not have all to leave!"

Her son Lancelot Minor Blackford was headmaster of the Episcopal high school for forty years. His son, John Minor Blackford, sent his son, William Blackford, from Seattle to Virginia to attend this school. This fact, and his attendance at the University of Virginia, leads Capt. William Blackford's son, Dr. Mansel Blackford, to surmise that his father was familiar with his abolitionist great-grandmother. Her thinking may have continued to influence the family. Dr. Blackford says, "My father was not a crusader." Still, Mary Berkeley Minor Blackford's portrait hung over the mantle of the Blackford family home. Perhaps a crusader is exactly what the *Mason* crew did not want. "He treated us man to man," was the judgment of more than one crew member.

Captain Blackford was promoted from the command of the *Mason* to duty at Great Lakes. When the war ended, he applied to join the regular navy, but his physical condition, particularly his weight, disqualified him. The entrance application had a remarks section that requested information about his "background which would be pertinent to his future assignment." He wrote about his experience in the adverse weather conditions of the Aleutians and then added this sentence, "Have escorted eight transatlantic convoys." No elaboration. No description of his crew as different than any other, just a summary of his responsibility: "Command and morale of crew."

Bill Farrell, from Chicago, was the engineering officer on the *Mason*. His self-identification probably rests more directly on his being an engineer than on being white. He spoke about his experiences from his hospital room. His love of the engine room on the *Mason* and his memory of the camaraderie of the men who served there seemed to strengthen him. The energetic "Steady Eddie" the men had described emerged as he spoke.

Bill Farrell: I was assigned to the DE-529, the USS *Mason*. While we were waiting for the crew to assemble, I stayed down in Florida to take several different courses. I took "Navy Courts and Boards," which is why I was assigned to the *Mason* as senior member of the Summary Court Martial Board. I was also the chief engineer, recreation officer, athletics officer, and welfare officer because it was a small ship.

At that time it was to be a white crew on the *Mason*, but one day we were called in by the navy people in Florida and told that the navy had decided to put a black crew on the ship.

We were asked for our comments at that time, asked what we thought. We were already a fairly close nucleus of people. There were probably eight officers altogether in Florida. We told them that we would like to think about it, to talk among ourselves. The only reason we did that was because we had this one fellow from Texas, and we didn't want him to be the only one who might say "no." The navy told us that it wouldn't be held against us if we chose not to go on the *Mason*.

We decided that we'd all say "yes" or all say "no." We talked about it with all the officers. Kitts, the guy from Texas, had no objection at all! So we told them okay, we'd take it. The navy did not want a person who was prejudiced serving on the ship. As a matter of fact, we had to sign some sort of a document that stated we were given the opportunity of not accepting these orders, that we were taking them, and that we had no prejudice about the whole thing (see Appendix B). So that was fine.

Blackford (letter to his parents): USS MASON (DE 529) 15 January 1944: Pre-commissioning work is progressing slowly but steadily and every day shortens the time when Jane and I will part. The volume of detail work is terrific and I am sure if all the printed forms were utilized for fuel the ship could sail around the world. We have a good office force of about 30 men set-up here, but most of the crew are still at training school. They are doing very well according to all reports (one is enclosed—please mail it back). Am delighted with the colored men who are here now—they know what they are doing and can really put out the work. We are setting up a ship's band which will be something, as many of the men have had band experience and the Navy will provide instruments.

Graham: While in Boston, waiting to go aboard the *Mason*, we were billeted in the Fargo Building. I really did enjoy the base. I had no trouble with white sailors on base, but off the base, white American sailors in the continental United States, Europe, Africa—any place we met—always had some derogatory remarks about my race, which I am very proud of, or my ship, which I have always been proud of. Returning from liberty one night in Boston, walking towards the main gate, I asked a white sailor, "What ship are you from mate?" He replied, the USS *Bermingham* (which happened to be the *Mason*'s sister ship). I said that I was from the USS *Mason*.

"Oh, that's the nigger ship," he said. The fight was on. We both had on white uniforms. When the fight was over we both were a bloody mess. He was the loser. The whole time we were fighting the marine guard watched, but he didn't utter a sound or make any moves!

Blackford (letter to his parents): USS MASON (DE 529) 15 January 1944: It will probably be the middle of March before we finally get away from here for shakedown, though possibly two weeks sooner. Will be under Commander Atlantic Destroyers for a while—then a long trip Westward.

The *Mason* was supposed to be sent to the Pacific and, in fact, was even painted with jungle camouflage. But the events of the summer of 1944 changed her direction. She would escort convoys supplying the D-Day invasion and its aftermath.

Blackford (letter to his parents): USS MASON (DE 529) 15 January 1944: Am very much pleased with the ship. (Should be!—cost $7,000,000.) We have all the scientific gadgets aboard that can be put in the space available. Will have 12 officers and around 200 men. We are about 300 feet in length and quite good looking with streamlined bridge and stack, etc. Our armament, though not too heavy, should prove effective for the type of work for which we are designed. Our evaporation will provide all the fresh water that anyone could possibly use aboard. The Quarters are ample but certainly not lavish. I have a private bath and quarters separate from the rest of the wardroom officers' cabins. We are fortunate in having quite a few experienced officers aboard—from all parts of the world. As far as fighting experience goes the exec, Lt. Commander Ed O. Ross, is well acquainted with the busy ports along this coast having had command of an Atlantic P.C. which operated for a time in the Mediterranean during some hot action. Was worried about the East Coast for a while because most of the skippers around here know all the channels into the different ports, from experience.

Farrell: I was a fairly young engineer, and I *loved* the equipment in the engine room. It was beautiful. I had these big diesels to run the generators and make power. They drove these big motors, 1,500-horsepower motors. When the ship went on commission, it was so pretty down there. All the engines were painted this gray; navy gray I guess they call it, battleship gray. I remember the ship's service switchboard was canary yellow, with brown around the meters and trims. The propulsion board was beige. The bulkheads were all white, and the bilges were zinc chromate. Everything was so beautiful. I resolved right then that that was the way the engine room was going to stay. It was going to look just like that when we decommissioned it. And it did.

Sometimes we'd have a little engine trouble and have to work four to six hours getting things back in condition. Of course, there'd be a lot of mess around, a lot of oil and grease on the bulkheads. But we weren't finished repairing the engines until we washed down all the bulkheads on the thing. It was good.

Graham: When we went aboard, we didn't have hot water, we didn't have running water. There were plumbers, electricians, and lines all over the ship when we went aboard. But I was there. I was aboard the *Mason!*

The composition of the crew of the *Mason* made the commissioning of the ship newsworthy.

New York Times (3/21/44): NEW NAVY CREW MOSTLY NEGRO— (Boston, March 20)—The destroyer-escort *Mason*, first United States naval vessel with a predominantly Negro crew, was commissioned today at Boston Navy Yard. The crew of 204 includes forty-four whites. Later the vessel will be manned entirely by Negroes specially trained for destroyer-escort duty. The *Mason* was named for Ensign Newton H. Mason, a hero of the battle of the Coral Sea, and was sponsored by his mother, Mrs. David N. Mason, Scarsdale, N.Y.

The press in the black community saw the event in broader terms.

Atlanta Daily News: FIRST RACE-MANNED WAR SHIP IN SERVICE— (Boston)—With a cold bitter wind accompanying a steady snowfall on this first day of spring the first U.S. Naval vessel with a predominantly Negro crew, the Destroyer Escort USS *Mason,* was placed in full commission Monday at Boston Navy Yard by Captain Roman C. Grady, U.S.N., captain of the yard.

This is the larger of the two new anti-submarine vessels with crews largely composed of Negroes.

Lieutenant Commander William M. Blackford, USNR, of Seattle, Washington, assumed command of the ship as soon as Captain Grady published the commissioning orders of the navy department. His crew presently consists of 160 Negroes and 44 whites. It is anticipated that as soon as Negro personnel can be trained and qualified they will replace the white ratings in their specialized billets, so that the entire crew eventually will be Negroes.

Governor Saltonstall and Mayor Tobin spoke briefly after the impressive ceremony as did Julian D. Steele, director of the Armstrong Hemenway Foundation and local president of the NAACP, who previously had presented the crew with a number of musical instruments, for which he was warmly thanked.

The parents of the late Ensign Newton Henry Mason, USNR, pilot of the Coral Sea battle for whom vessel was named, were also present and Mrs. Mason presented a plaque and picture of her son to the ship, following the commissioning. Their home is in Scarsdale, New York.

There was a moistness in the eyes of some of the colored workers who with their white comrades braved the bitter cold to witness the ceremony but above and beyond all a note of pride, for absenteeism is low among them and they had kept this secret.

They sensed that not only was this something they had helped fashion with their own hands and skill to be manned by their own boys but that this was their opportunity to show the world they were just as capable under a welder's hood as machine gunning an enemy plane and just as efficient at turning lathe as running down an enemy submarine.

Blackford (commissioning speech): Governor Saltonstall, Admiral Theobold, Captain Grady, Mayor Tobin, officers and crew of the USS *MASON*, ladies and gentlemen. The Commander in Chief desires that the following letter be read to the men of the *MASON*:

FROM: The Secretary of the Navy
TO: Commanding Officer, USS *MASON* (DE-529)
SUBJECT: Readiness for War Service

1. The Secretary of the Navy congratulates you, your officers and crew on being assigned to duty in the USS *MASON*. He takes this occasion to impress on each of you the seriousness and importance of your responsibilities in the days and weeks ahead.
2. Immediately after her shaking down period, the USS *MASON* will be assigned to duty wherever she is then most needed. It is entirely possible that you will proceed directly into combat. Your first action may be by day or by night, against any type of vessel or aircraft possessed by our able and ruthless enemies.
3. The only training period assured to you is from now until [the time] you report to the USS *MASON* ready for duty. Take full advantage of every facility and every hour to attain maximum readiness for war during your shakedown.
4. Your future Fleet, Force, and Unit Commanders must rely on the USS *MASON* as an effective fighting unit from the hour when she reports to them for duty. It is your task to justify their confidence.

FRANK KNOX

I am fully cognizant of the responsibilities entailed in assuming command of this ship. I am sure that we are off to a good start. Most of you have been to sea before in local defense craft and small ships. You have been selected to man the USS *MASON* on the basis of previous meritorious service. You have demonstrated to me your ability and desire to learn by the excellent manner in which you have tackled the job of outfitting and preliminary training here at Boston and at Norfolk. The real job is just beginning. It will only be after months of hard work and ceaseless drills that we can attain that degree of fighting efficiency required of a first line ship.

Ensign Newton Henry Mason, for whom the ship was named, has given his life in a fearless devotion to duty. For this he was posthumously awarded the Distinguished Flying Cross. Ensign Mason was awarded the American Defense Service Medal (Fleet Clasp) 1939–1941, and the DISTINGUISHED FLYING CROSS with the following citation: "For extraordinary achievement in serial combat as pilot of a fighter plane in action against enemy Japanese forces in the Battle of the Coral Sea on May 7 and 8, 1942. With utter disregard for his own personal safety, Ensign

Mason zealously engaged enemy Japanese aircraft, thus contributing materially to the defense of our forces. In this action he gallantly gave up his life in the service of his country." We are very proud to carry his name.

Now I wish to especially thank Captain Grady and the Boston Navy Yard organization on behalf of the officers and crew of the *MASON* for the excellent start they have given us. The well-organized Supply Department and Pre-Commissioning Detail, as well as the planning and various construction departments, have greatly facilitated the job of getting the ship ready for duty. We wish to thank the civilian yard employees for carrying out the unusually high standards of construction which are apparent in this ship. We also wish to thank Dr. & Mrs. Mason and our other guests for being with us today. Your interest in the USS *MASON* is sincerely appreciated.

Blackford (letter to his parents): USS MASON (DE 529) 23 March 1944: Well, the big doings are over now and we are down to hard work. The commissioning went off perfectly in the middle of a snowstorm [see Appendix C]. I certainly couldn't keep up with the Mayor and Governor in speech making but think I held my own anyway. Dr. and Mrs. Mason gave us a plaque and oil portrait of Ensign Mason for our wardroom. A colored society gave us enough musical instruments to form a ship's band.

Farrell: I was recreation officer, and we decided we were going to have a ball for the crew to celebrate the commissioning. We went around and had a little committee set up. I invited the governor of Massachusetts and the mayor of Boston, and both of them came to our pre-commissioning ball on the *Mason*.

Someone on the crew knew about a school in a suburb of Boston, a finishing school for black girls. Most of our guys were from out of town; they didn't really know people around Boston. So we invited girls from the school down for the pre-commissioning ball. They attended the ball, beautiful girls, dressed to the teeth. We had a nice party.

DuFau: Commissioning was such a regular event in that navy area, they probably had connections with all of the local organizations. But I remember there was a ballroom where the regular enlisted men *and* the officers used to go.

Graham: The day that we had the commissioning, it was so cold.

DuFau: It was *icy* cold.

Graham: We were anxious to hit the beach to get on liberty, and a lot of us didn't hang around for any kind of dance. I know I didn't. That's when the photographer wanted certain color caps put on. I happened to have on a blue cap. When he said he wanted a blue cap, we all raced back to the lower deck and got on white caps, in order to get off the ships right away.

Blackford (letter to his parents): USS MASON (DE 529) 23 March 1944: It feels pretty good to be back on a ship at last, especially a real warship. We have started out by observing all the regular customs and ceremonies aboard ship, as our crew seems to like things a little more that way than other DE's. With this many in the crew they can't all be good though, and I was forced to hold a couple of courts today. A lot of this strict way of doing things is fairly new to me but we are off to a good start. I believe that by bearing down a little more than necessary at first we can ease up later. I think that the crew is better than average and is developing some spirit. There has been a lot of bunk said about Negro crews. We can't see that they are any different from others if treated the same, but will know more later. They are anxious to make a name for themselves. [They] actually work harder. It's quite obviously a good change for me if it works out as I expect.

Now the men could actually walk on their ship and get to know other crew members. They waited for the ship to be ready for the shakedown cruise.

Buchanan: We had about forty white crew members, noncoms. All of the officers at one point were white. And we had about 160 black sailors. We manned all of the positions, all of the ranks: radiomen, signalmen, quartermasters, sonar men, motor machinists. Some people came aboard radio third class, but when they left they were chief petty officers—quite a few of them.

Garrison: There was another ship, a smaller one, with a black crew, called the *1264*. But this ship didn't go overseas like we did. They ran up and down the coast. I think they went to the Caribbean a couple of times. But the *Mason* was the very first warship with a predominantly black crew that the navy ever commissioned. Destroyer escort or any ship, really.

Peters: I went aboard that ship with stars in my eyes. This was a great opportunity. It fit in more with what I wanted to do, as opposed to maybe just sitting on some base somewhere, having a sedentary job. It was an opportunity for travel, for adventure— all of the usual things that an eighteen-year-old has in mind.

The *Mason* was challenging. I went aboard as a rated person, which was quite different from going aboard without a rate. I had already proven myself, so I didn't have a lot to prove when I got there.

Grant: We were handpicked, all of the black and white guys: 180 black and about 40 white. We were all handpicked from throughout the navy, all bases.

Divers: We were called "Eleanor's Folly." The whole nation was pushed by Eleanor Roosevelt. It wasn't only the *Mason*, there were other integrated outfits in the other services—the Ninety-Ninth Pursuit Squadron, called the Tuskegee Airmen, and others. But I think the powers that be that opposed integration had programmed us to fail. The USS *Mason* was not expected to succeed. But when we started proving them wrong and succeeding, rather than eat crow, they downplayed all our accomplishments and all our virtues.

But the ship's log didn't. The official record of their service began on commissioning day. The war diary summarized each day's events, while the deck log reported on each four-hour watch. On April 3, 1944, Lt. Charles M. Dillon—in compliance with Bureau of Naval Personnel orders—came aboard to observe the black crewmen. (Dillon later served in the navy's special program's unit and played a central role in reversing the discriminatory policies of the navy.)

DuFau: You had these people, observers, come aboard; they were personnel officers. But we knew they were there to see how we'd do. And we were fully aware that we would be under the microscope, and we realized the load that was on us. And looking back, I'm glad I didn't know as much then as I know now, because I probably would have been shaken up a bit to know what weight we had to carry. But it was a puzzle to me why we had to be studied like something in a laboratory. We were human beings, blood running in our veins, loyal American citizens doing everything that was required. You know, living by the rules and everything. But when it came to working in the service, all of a sudden we were only qualified to serve meals or do just menial stuff. But the weight of proving our ability was on us and opening the doors for those who would come behind. It was really a double front that we were up against.

Garrison: Apart from some people thinking that we couldn't do the job, I think the whole basis of segregation itself was that you had to mingle and be close to each other. On a ship, you're sleeping here, I'm sleeping there. That's what I think people objected to more than anything else. I don't think they doubted that we could do the job, but to do the job, you had to have that close association. And a lot of the white sailors and those in command were not willing to have that. So I think that's what it really was.

Farrell: Shortly after she was commissioned, we took her down to Bermuda on shakedown. We didn't go on shakedown twice, we went once. But you usually stay on shakedown for a month. We stayed a week or two longer, but that had nothing to do with the crew needing any more training than anyone else. What gave me gray hairs was the evaporator. It was the sole piece of equipment that you had only one of on the ship. And when the evaporator was down, you would suddenly get thirsty. I think all of the DEs really had problems with them on shakedown.

That was the first time we got away from the public water supplies, but the crew would still go in and turn the shower on full force, and just bathe there for a long while. And we had to make all that water. We could make less than four thousand gallons a day, and the crew was over two hundred people, so we ran pretty short. Down in Bermuda, where we had the shakedown, there's no water. During peacetime they used to lug the water down from New York. What you depend on for water down there normally is the rainwater collected into cisterns. If you ran out of water, you would have to go to the commander of the area there and explain that your ship didn't have any water. I used to tell the crew, "I am not going to go over there and beg for water. We've got to learn how to live on it."

We did pretty good, really, but I knew the crew wanted showers. We put in saltwater showers on the deck, because we had a lot of that. But the crew didn't want the saltwater showers; they wanted the freshwater showers.

Divers: You've got to remember, we had almost three hundred guys on a small ship. And we had to be clean. We couldn't afford to be untidy. When we caught a guy who even halfway didn't smell right, we'd give him a G.I. bath with a big, stiff brush, and we'd almost take the skin off of him with salt water. He got the message pretty fast.

We kept our ship clean and tidy and our personal health up to snuff. We saw to that. You had to in a ship, with that many guys in a ship that small.

Graham: Our quarters were down below—just about at the waterline. Our bunks folded up against the side, and we'd sleep in tiers. So, if you came in from watch and someone was in his sack, you'd have to wake him up to pull down your bunk. Some compartments became mess halls during the day. Our head was just a trough that water flowed down. There were wooden slat things that fit over the trough so you could sit down, with room for about ten.

During her shakedown period the observers from the navy's Bureau of Personnel watched the *Mason* closely. "Re-fueling, towing, hedgehog, gunnery and underwater exercises were satisfactorily performed and the ship was well handled in day and night maneuvers" (44). There was only one area that the bureau seemed extremely concerned about—cleanliness. The report's discussion of the *Mason's* shakedown cruise (and later of her convoy service) devotes more space to scrubbing the decks than the real achievement of the ship. Interestingly, though, the observers traced some of this deficiency to the *white* chief petty officers assigned to the ship, who were not performing their duties well. Their behavior was seemingly excused because they "were not volunteers for the duty. . . . there was evidence that the white petty officers in general did not like their duty and apparently accepted it primarily with the hope that it meant more rapid advancement in ratings (an expectation lacking in foundation)" (43).

Happily for the *Mason* crew, their captain shared the attitudes they themselves had: ignore the naysayer and get on with the job at hand. Let the observers poke and prod; let the navy worry about dust on footlockers; we have a war to win. While in Bermuda, Captain

Blackford demonstrated a willingness to, when necessary, ignore the navy's petitioners, which would endear him to his men. The bureau's report described one such incident in Bermuda. "At the request of the DE-DD Shakedown Task Group Commander, no liberty was granted the MASON's crew during the scheduled period of exercises. This was a discrimination, since crews from other ships present were granted liberty; but the inequality of course caused special resentment among the Negro personnel, with whom the issue of discrimination is always particularly sensitive" (44). (Not to mention the "issue" of liberty, which seems "particularly sensitive" for all sailors!)

The report goes on: "Finally during the MASON's fifth and last week in the area, the Commanding Officer wisely took it upon himself to grant liberty. The ship's liberty parties were well behaved" (44). Whatever the problems with the white chiefs, the man in charge was someone the crew knew would stand up for them, and under his leadership, the ship's crew began to coalesce.

DuFau: Once the other ships found out who we were, it always was this *challenge* situation. We were on a training trip as part of the shakedown. We were pretending to be escorting a convoy. For some reason or another, we had to be the center of communications. I think four or five ships were sending signals to us by signal light at the same time. Some officer looked over the side and wanted to know, "DuFau, what the heck's going on down there?"

Without thinking, I told him, "Shut up!"

The thing stayed in my mind. I said, "Oh, God, I told an officer to shut up." But he stayed quiet. He wanted to know what the heck we were doing down there. It seemed like confusion, you know, all these ships flashing lights at us. And I told him, "Every one of them is under control." We were using anybody we could grab to record the signals. Guys from the C-Division, for example, used to be up on the bridge, hanging out. And we would make them recorders because we had only four signalmen. So we would use the other guys as recorders. And we did it. We relayed all those signals. Later on our trips we would teach them all the code. I remember the radiomen practicing with flashlights.

War Diary (20 April 1944): USS MASON (DE 529) Narrative Remarks: Completed fourteen (14) simulated depth charges attacks. Allowed seven hits by spotters. Various other scheduled and unscheduled exercises conducted. Operations conducted with USS HAYTER (DE 212) and SS VORTICE.

War Diary (21 April 1944): USS MASON (DE 529) Narrative Remarks: Underway at 0648 for A.S.W. (Anti Submarine Warfare) exercise with Italian submarine using advanced evasive tactics. Fired patterns of four (4) plaster loaded Mark 10 projectiles each run. Echo ranging condition very poor limiting number of runs for the day to eleven. Five hits scored.

Garrison: Teamwork is especially important. Every man must be a specialist in what he does. You have no fire department, so if a fire breaks out, you have to know how to put it out. We had collision drills. We had abandon-ship drills. We would drill so much that you could do it just at the snap of the fingers.

Watkins: I heard about the *Mason* when she was on her shakedown, but I also heard, "Don't volunteer for anything!"—so I didn't. I went home that evening, and coming back on the train to Great Lakes there was another guy with me who said, "You know, I think maybe we're goofy if we don't volunteer for the *Mason*. Let's go at lunchtime and sign up."

I said, "All right." But before we could, the word came over, "Watkins, report to the office." And that was it. I was assigned to the *Mason*.

I had left all of my clothes at home because I was more or less commuting to Great Lakes from my home on the south side. But I was told, "Catch the train; you're going to New York." I lived way out on the south side of Chicago, and it was kind of rough to get my things and get back to the station. I remember running for the train with my wife. She was working at Palmer House and she ran to meet me at the train. Then we were both running down the tracks to catch the train!

The *Mason* had left on her shakedown, so they sent me to Norfolk, then to Charleston, to try to catch the ship. Finally, I got aboard ship, and the engineering officer said he needed three guys. A guy named Cook—we called him Big Cook—said to me, "Take the job, take the job."

That's how I got in the E-division (they called engineering E-division). I learned about the engines and the evaporators.

First I worked in the after engine room—that was fine. But the engine room itself was terrible. On the first voyage, I was pretty seasick, and the engine room didn't help at all! It got pretty hot. But we survived. And then they wanted a striker for the guy in charge of fuel and oil—they called him the oil king. So I became the striker for the oil king and, eventually, the oil king myself.

We did maintenance on board too so that we wouldn't have to do it after we were in port.

Garrison: But as much progress as we were making on board ship, we still had to face the outside. After the shakedown we were in port at Norfolk, I think. On the Chesapeake Bay ferry they had a snack bar. I was sitting with a shipmate who was white. I ordered something, and the woman served me. But then a man came out and told me I had to get up and leave. At that point, some of my shipmates, who were white, were ready to turn the place out. But I asked them not to do it. Because see, coming from the South, I knew what would happen. They wouldn't care whether you were white, black, purple, or green—something would happen. And so I just left it there.

Gordon: Only once did I ever have any real problems from the guys in the ship. I was talking to a white guy about this not long ago, about being categorized black. He was white. His response was, "Well, a little dab will do it." I don't know who set these rules. My percentage of Negro blood was one-sixteenth, and that was enough to make me a Negro.

But racism didn't go in the reverse in those days. Black people were so used to being mistreated, it never occurred to them to mistreat anybody else.

That's how I found it once I was mixed with the black crew. The guys never gave me too much trouble, except when we were in Charleston, South Carolina. The ship was not welcome there. The first night on liberty there was some kind of a riot. Here were all of these black sailors running around with rating badges. This was not something seen down there. The rest of the navy was black servants, period. The guys got in a fight ashore, and when they came back to the ship, they were ready to kill. I mean, they were very angry. And three of them came to my bunk and said, "We want some white blood" (of course, they had been drinking).

I just boldly told them, "Well, you're not going to get it here." But I was very scared, because I thought anything could happen. But being a shipmate—we'd been at sea and we'd been through the shakedown cruise and everything—I was one of the guys, so that didn't turn into anything.

I have had my share of racism from both sides of the table, but I don't recognize racism, period. To me, it's the ultimate in ignorance to consider somebody by the color of their skin. The men of the *Mason* ranged from real black to myself, in all shades. We were just human beings. The navy did not consider us just human beings, and that's why we were treated as some kind of an experiment or something. I never did understand why, because I went to mixed schools, and I never found anybody in schools that was smarter than I was. In my classes, nobody ever got higher grades than I did. So to me, I never considered myself limited. Of course, the obvious response to that was that I didn't have enough black blood in me! But I found that the sailors on the *Mason* were as smart as, and a lot of them a lot smarter than, I was—so it had nothing to do with color.

I have been very offended by the way the men on the *Mason* were treated because of the color of their skin, as though they were something less than human.

Watkins: I didn't know anything about segregation. I'd heard about it, but I hadn't experienced it. The first time was in Norfolk, I think. A guy named Johnson, from Oregon, and I caught the ferry. I said, "Johnson, look at all the black dudes over here." It turned out, we were on the wrong side of the ferry!

And still I didn't get it. We went down the street, and we saw this pretty little girl sitting by the orange-aid cooler in a restaurant. We decided to go in there. "We'll have some of that orange-aid," we told her.

This redneck came in behind us. "Yeah, but you'll drink it outside!"

She said, "I can't serve you here."

So I said, "Well . . ." but the guy behind us growled, so we said, "Okay. Bye-bye." Then I said, "Johnson, you're from Portland, Oregon, and I'm from Chicago. Look what we're getting into!"

Then there was the bus. If we were going into Charleston or into any other town, they'd stop in the city and collect the fare. One time the bus was loaded, and I was sitting by the window, a white sailor sitting next to me. The driver said to the white sailor, "You'll have to get up or I won't move the bus."

The white sailor started to argue, but I said, "Hey, kid, go sit over there. We don't want to get into anything we can't win."

We were fairly angry, but there wasn't a win for us. The drivers made sure before they got into town that everybody was seated properly, and then they'd collect the fares.

It puzzled me that they didn't want you to sit side by side on the bus, but you could live side by side in the housing there, in Charleston, in Norfolk, in *all* of them. That was the thing that bothered me.

I remember there was a transfer in a town in Virginia, and we stopped for awhile. One of the guys said, "Hey, let's go get some beer." So we go into this place, and we go through the kitchen, and here's a big black cook.

"Where are you guys going?" he asked.

We said, "We want to go get some beer."

"All right. What do you want? What do you want?"

I said, "You mean I can't get it to take it out?"

"No, I have to get it for you."

"You keep it," I said and I busted outdoors. The rest of the guys stayed there. They got back and they were opening the beer on the train. Finally they said, "Oh, we bought you one. We knew you didn't have sense enough to know what was going on down there."

DuFau: Integration had *begun* when I went in in '42. But it really took an order from Truman in '48. He put his foot down. My understanding was that in the beginning they were going to train us and then eventually integrate. But that process was going on at such a slow speed. Even with a commander in chief behind you, by the time the order goes down to the little guy who has you isolated on a ship somewhere, they can do what they want to do. And then, by the time the chain of command hears from you, you may be in trouble for just going over his head and making a complaint.

Peters: The one thing that sticks out in my mind was down in South Carolina, right in this country. The Red Cross was coming through to the various ships that were docked down there. They were distributing doughnuts, candy, and coffee to all the other ships around us, and they skipped our ship. I mean, it was blatant. They stopped and they took care of the ship behind us, and then they proceeded past our ship to the next ship.

Now, I was a very rebellious person. The first time I saw colored and white water fountains, I purposely got off the ship and went to the white drinking fountain. So I was really angry!

Everybody aboard the ship was irate about it. There wasn't a lot we could do. I just thought, "I will not support the Red Cross. If the Red Cross can act this way toward us, then why should I contribute money?"

Garrison: When we went aboard the *Mason* there were some petty officers who were white. We never had any problems with them though, except for the chief radioman; he was somewhat hard to get along with. I don't think there were any problems with the rest of them. There was no such thing as open hostility. I never sensed that.

DuFau: The hostility aboard the ship didn't come out. First of all there were so many black guys, our world was each other. There were a few white enlisted men; most of them were chiefs. They were supposed to instruct us. Some had an attitude. You just sensed when there wasn't a calm. Whenever a chief petty officer was hostile to us, you could just feel it. At our age, we weren't dumb; we knew you don't have to say everything. It was body language, the way an order was given and all that. We could just feel who was who, but we knew the captain was with us, and that really helped.

Garrison: I really liked the insistence on professionalism, the constant training, always training, drilling, making sure that you did what you did and that you knew how to do it. In the navy you depended upon each other so strongly. It's teamwork. And that's why I think we never had any problems, because we realized that if I did my job as I should and he did his, we would all get it done. We were very proud of what we did.

You see, a ship at sea is self-contained. You don't have a fire department. If a fire breaks out, you have to know how to put it out. We didn't have a doctor aboard; we had a corps-man, a pharmacist's mate. The idea was, you had to do every-thing. Every man knew just what he had to do, and he did his job. You could depend upon each other. That's what I liked about it.

For some drills they would use stopwatches to see how quickly we could get it done. Sometimes the chief said, "Do it over." He said he once saw a destroyer just disintegrate in thirty seconds, and only those who were topside survived. If you didn't get out quickly enough, that would be it.

Maiden Voyage

At last the *Mason* was under way, doing what all the training had been aimed at—escorting a convoy across the Atlantic. These were the first black navy men to take a warship into battle in foreign waters. Racist presumptions about their inability to operate a modern warship while under enemy fire could be dispelled. This voyage was so important to the black community that Thomas W. Young, a black journalist whose family owned the *Journal and Guide of Norfolk*, asked to make the voyage. He became the first black war correspondent to report from a U.S. Navy warship. His articles were reprinted by black newspapers in every city. Young knew that history was being made, and while his dispatches focus on the specific—individual men, the duties they perform, the family life of the *Mason* at sea—there is a sense of the momentous. "The USS Mason Goes to War—History Is Made" reads one headline.

As the *Mason* headed for the open sea, the young men in her crew were not thinking of themselves as symbols or pioneers. Their attention was on present dangers and the excitement of the adventure ahead. They were crossing thousands of miles of ocean in one of the smallest of the navy's warships. The sea itself was a formidable enemy, and under that sea lurked German U-boats manned by experienced crews dedicated to destroying the ships of the convoy.

Each day at dawn general quarters sounded on the *Mason*, shaking the young sailors from the tiers of bunks crowded below deck. In the rush topside no man knew for sure if this was the routine morning call or a submarine contact. U-boats favored dawn and dusk for attack. Even if no human enemy threatened, there was the sea itself, which, as C. S. Forester wrote in his story of a World War II convoy *The Good Shepherd*, "extended for a thousand miles and beneath it the water was two miles deep." Such figures, he went on, are not "easily grasped by the imagination though acceptable as academic fact."

The crews of the destroyer escorts knew they were to protect the larger ships at the cost of their own. They were the shepherds, and like the good shepherd of the parable, they were expected to lay down their lives for their sheep. But they were also the sheepdogs charged to round up straggling ships, nipping at the heels of the bigger ships, bringing them into line. Conventional sea wisdom said that thirty to forty ships of different types and capabilities could not be kept moving together at the same speed by the sheepdogs. Yet they were. And if a wolf threatened the flock, the DEs would drive him off, kill him, or offer themselves as a distraction so that the convoy would be spared. The new radar and sonar equipment signaled when a U-boat threatened, and by applying formulas based on the work of Albert Einstein and his fellow physicists at Princeton, the DEs could find out where the wolf packs were hiding. Then a thousand more human calculations followed: How far away was the contact? Was there enough fuel to reach it? Should it be scared away or attacked? Was it one U-boat or a member of a wolf pack? These calculations were made in seconds. Every man had to know his job and respond immediately. Turn the wheel a few degrees in the wrong direction, misread a signal flag, receive a message incorrectly, or misinterpret a sonar contact, and the entire convoy would be jeopardized. These men who took the *Mason* across the ocean eight times do not inflate their experiences. They see their ship simply as one of the five hundred DEs that shepherded convoys and hunted submarines. They were young. A sense of their own immortality tempered fear and blunted their sense of danger. Now they marvel at their casual bravery. They were "young and foolish, young and goofy," they say. But they were confident and glad to depend on each other's skill and ability.

They were taking the *Mason* out beyond the limitations imposed by segregation and racism into this expanse of sea and sky. This was what the *Mason* was to them, a ship at sea, and they were her crew. Let the navy worry about studies and experiments and measuring black against white. They were 160 young men who knew they were good at what they did. They respected their captain and could ignore slights from the few white chief petty officers who wished they weren't there. They were there. The *Mason* was their ship.

Maybe it was a small ship and maybe escort duty was not considered a glamorous assignment by others in the fleet, but the crew knew if they got the oil tanker across, then tanks could fight and troops could move and bombers could fly. When they brought a cargo ship to port, medicine, clothes, and food became available for GIs and civilians alike. No one better underestimate the *Mason* or speak against it. A poem written by one of the crewmen sums up the feelings of his shipmates this way:

So when you meet up with the *Mason*
Please select your chatter well
For if you should use some slander, Jack
You've got a home in hell.

War Diary (1 July 1944): USS MASON (DE 529) underway in company with DE's 187, 188, 528, USS JOHN M. BERMINGHAM (DE 530) comprising task group 27.5, escorting convoy CK-3 via Bermuda and Azores. At present, en route Bermuda to Horta (Azores). . . . Patrolling sector on port bow of convoy.

DuFau: The destroyer escort was really a fragile ship, according to standards of navy vessels. The hull was very thin metal. But they had to get vessels out there to counteract the submarines, to escort convoys. To do it the quickest way, they had to sacrifice certain safety features. The destroyer escort wound up being able to do the job.

Now, I wasn't crazy about water. I had never seen that much water. The widest body of water I saw was Lake Pontchartrain in Louisiana. I never did see to the other side of it. But then to get on the ocean and be traveling for days and not see land, and then look on the charts and get an idea of how far we had traveled and how far we *had* to travel before we'd see land, that was an amazing thing, especially knowing how fragile the ship was. That little ship in the midst of all that water.

Divers: I made all six trips with the *Mason* overseas. I had the privilege of being on the flying bridge, where I could monitor all the information on the TBS, talk between ships, and also the intercoms on board our own ship. I was privy to a lot of information the other guys didn't have. I would hear the commodore who was in charge of the whole convoy talk to the other ships. I could hear him getting on the other ships about maintaining station. "Maintain station. Get on station." But we never had that problem. We always were on station. That was Blackford's doing. He insisted that his officers stay on station.

Buchanan: I knew that when you were going on convoys to Europe you were in dangerous waters. I knew that. But I could survive that. In fact, I was known around the ship as not one to worry about going into the water. It took them a long time to even make me wear a life jacket! I'd say, "I'm up thirty-three feet, forty feet, and if I jump into the water, I don't want any life jacket on because it will break my neck." The life jacket will snap your neck right off. I used to tie my life jacket up high on the mast. When I'd get to the signal bridge, during GQ, I could reach up and get mine. But the life jacket was no guarantee.

War Diary (3 July 1944): Patrolling on port bow of convoy. . . . 1213–Sighted empty life raft. 1305–Radar contact, bearing 115 degrees True, 34,000 yards–No IFF. Target tracked on collision course with convoy speed twenty-five (25) knots. At 1325, target visible, exchanged recognition signals and call signs, reporting same to escort commander. Target proved to be H.M.S. BIRMINGHAM. At 1416, USS POWERS (DE 528) report submarine contact. All ships steamed to area. Contact apparently false. At 2028, conducted forty (40) minute battle problem.

Gordon Buchanan recognized the British ship the *Birmingham*, but the significance of the empty life jacket and abandoned life raft was there for *all* to see.

Buchanan: In the service school for destroyer escort crews they give you a test to see if you can recognize ships. I got a 4.0 on the test. Not only did I recognize the kind of ship, I could give you the *name;* I had *that* much definition. And that was in my records aboard ship, because they made me a recognitions officer even though I was only a petty officer. I spotted the *Birmingham*—funny the HMS *Birmingham* passing the USS *Bermingham*, a DE with us! But we always used to get information in about the enemy's ships or planes. I had to teach it to the crew. I didn't teach the whole ship at a time. I'd get several guys down, put all the pictures out and show them, and explain it. If intelligence had found out about an airplane that the Germans or the Japanese had, I would explain that to them. I was recognitions officer aboard that ship only because of that 4.0 on the test. It was all that model building I had done.

Grant: I was the captain's secretary. I did the reports, the ship's logs. I took it in shorthand and then typed it out. My office was right next to the captain's quarters. We had a beautiful relationship. I went on board as a yeoman third class and within eighteen months he had me made yeoman first class. That's unheard of, to go from third class to first class in eighteen months. This was not because he liked me or anything, it was because of the work I had done. He acted toward us as man to man. We all thought he was a great man. He understood human nature, how to deal with people. He didn't treat anyone as an inferior.

Gordon: As a sonar operator, I was trained to detect the existence of a target in the area. The targets ranged from a school of fish to bottom return—bottom echoes—and so forth. The sonar equipment sent out a sound transmission, which had a tone to it. The echo coming back would indicate that there was an object in the range of the sonar. Depending on whether that object was moving or not, it would give what was called Doppler. Doppler was the response and the tone of the return echo. With that, you could identify a moving target or a stationary target; you could identify whether it was a solid object or a school of fish.

Whales gave us a particular problem because they were solid enough and big enough to give us a good return. So in many cases we thought we had a submarine, and it would turn out to be a whale. Usually, when you were tracking a whale, sooner or later he blew. And when he blew, then you knew you had a whale.

Watkins: We were constantly changing course, screening, sounding—setting off sonar patterns. In a regular convoy the U-boats were up front and alongside. If you were on a big convoy and you straggled, you were out of luck. They couldn't afford to slow the whole convoy for one ship. I remember one time when they drove the convoy up in two separate segments, one for the slow ships and one for the fast ships. We had to pick up the guys behind until they'd try to catch up. You couldn't afford to wait on anybody out there.

Garrison: Remember, the sea is pitch-dark. You have no lights at *all.* The stars are very vivid because there's no artificial light.

But what amazes me is that with all the ships in the convoy in that pitch darkness, there were never any collisions.

DuFau: The fascinating thing was to go into the radio shack and see on the radar a picture of the whole convoy and see everything in position. You could identify those different locations and, as you say, it was fascinating to see everyone in line, changing course with no collisions.

Graham: Speaking of the dark nights, I used to stand at the fantail on those dark nights and look over the side at the wake, which was white so you could see it. Sometimes you'd see the phosphorus. I'd stand there watching that.

DuFau: Fish would dart through that water and through the phosphorus. It was beautiful, but you couldn't fully appreciate it because in the back of your mind, you knew you were at war. Still, the sea was beautiful when it was calm.

Graham: But those calm seas . . . I'd rather have the rough seas than the calm seas.

DuFau: A calm sea is too dangerous because you could be picked up too easily by the subs. They could see the wake of the ship.

Graham: In the rough seas you could hear the water whistling by, hitting you in the face—then you'd *feel* like a sailor. All I needed was a pipe.

Garrison: Did any of you guys get this feeling? When you're at sea and it's rough, you almost vow that you'll never go to sea again. And then when you go ashore and stay ashore for about two weeks, you're ready to go, you're eager to go back again.

DuFau: You can understand when people are talking about romance with the sea. You can fall in love with it.

Graham: When we were in those convoys, we'd see the other ships way off in the distance. We were together when we took on oil or passed the mail or exchanged movies. But we might go half a day and never see another ship.

Garrison: But the point is, we didn't collide. And that would have been *deadly*.

DuFau: Well, that was the great work of radar and men on watch. The lookouts were important. In case anything went haywire with your radar, your lookouts kept an eye on ships, how close they were. If they noticed any change in the course of a ship, they would call it to the attention of the deck officer. He was always there to relay word to the captain, if there was any danger.

But it was for the officer-of-the-deck to decide whether we were in danger. Human lookouts with their field glasses were important, as well as the radar, to hold the position.

Graham: The fear was that German wolf packs would come into the convoy. They would slip in and slip out, and they'd be in the middle of the configuration. Then you'd hear that a ship had been sunk. That was the danger.

The first landfall was in the Azore Islands, the halfway point for the convoy.

War Diary (7 July 1944): Anchored in twenty fathoms of water in Horta Roads, Azores. Fueled to capacity and returned to anchorage. Standing war cruising watches, listening watch and radar watch. Merchant ships of convoy anchored inshore of escorts. No liberty or shore leave allowed.

War Diary (8 July 1944): Anchored as before. Assigned shore patrol duties for the purpose of rounding up merchant seamen who had gotten ashore in bum boats.

Divers: We pulled into the Azores, a Portuguese possession, which at that time was neutral. They were a neutral colony, just like Argentina in South America. All ships could come in there; they had access to that port. And we came in at nighttime. The Portuguese port authority would meet and make sure that our depth charges were disarmed. This time we came in at night, and we tied up to a buoy. When daylight broke, what did we see but a German submarine.

Watkins: But we never went ashore. They wouldn't let us go to shore then. Remember?

Divers: No, they wouldn't let us go to shore.

Watkins: Then they sent some more green bananas over . . .

Divers: We're looking at the Germans, and they're looking at us.

Watkins: That didn't bother us.

Divers: They pulled anchor up and left, and the port authority wouldn't let us leave.

Watkins: It's good to be young. You don't worry. There were the German U-boats leaving port, and we knew they'd be out there in the ocean looking for us.

Divers: They would keep us for a certain amount of time after the U-boats left. We had to keep our distance. They've got a very big mountain, Pico, Mount Pico. You could see that mountain a whole day before you could even see the island, depending on how fast you were going. You could see that mountain sticking way up out of the ocean. And it would take you a whole day to get to it, you know, coming into the harbor. That's where the merchant marine guys jumped ship.

Watkins: Oh, yeah.

Divers: They jumped ship, and we sent a crew over to bring them back. I remember Big Woods was with them.

Watkins: Woods, that's who I was trying to think of.

Divers: Cook.

Watkins: Yeah, and Cook.

Divers: All those guys went over and went into the town and found the merchant marines. And the merchant marines said, "We're not sailing no more." Of course, I don't blame them. Those guys were dyin' like hell. All their ships were leaking; they didn't have fresh water or anything. But our guys had orders to bring them back and put 'em on the ship.

So the convoy started up again, with the *Mason* escorting merchant ships whose crews had to be forced back on board. At the Azores, almost as much ocean lay ahead as behind. They were entering areas favored by the U-boats; the communications division would be crucial to their safety.

Graham: On our maiden voyage to Ireland we had drills every step of the way. We were tracking submarines; there always seemed to be some kind of a GQ practice, or we'd be dropping depth charges.

I was a radio operator. As a matter of fact, I was in charge of the radio shack because I was the senior officer there. We would copy messages: most of them were from our own ships or from Washington, but sometimes we picked up German exchanges. We'd try to break them down.

Peters: I was fortunate to learn to read and interpret the German code. Because of this, I became a real key factor in the radio communication part of the ship. The wolf packs, German submarines that ran in packs, would surface at night to do their communication. I was able to intercept their messages and, in some respects, was able to break those messages to find out exactly where they were and what they were doing.

They didn't use the international Morse code; they had their own code. I hadn't learned this in the service school. I taught myself to copy the German code by listening to it. Just by listening to it and sorting it out. Once you become a radioman . . . It's a little hard to describe how you do this, but it becomes almost second nature to you. After you learned the international code, there were other codes that you could study, which is what I did. I began to pick those sounds up and was able to interpret what they were, what the letters were. Each letter was sent individually. We had encryptographic facilities that we could then go to and try to break whatever that code was to determine what the messages were.

I would turn the German messages over to the communications officer, who would take them to the captain. In most cases the reports were really position reports. We didn't get a lot of information aside from where they were located.

This was valuable information to our skipper and to the convoy in general. I can recall one time when I copied some German messages, and because they were so close to us, we put in to the Azore Islands, and we sat there for about a week, I believe. The German submarines *came in* while we were there. We watched them come in; they were on the surface when they came in. And they just waited us out. But then we slipped out and slipped away from them.

The skipper congratulated me, and there were some press reports on this.

Farrell: "Red-dog" was a name that started with Ed Ross. We'd be in convoys going across, and we'd get these messages. There would be two convoys ahead of us. A submarine would get in the convoy and sink some of the convoy, and maybe sink a DE. For some reason or other we'd call the submarine red-dog. The next night, or two nights later, we'd get another message: The sub had gotten into the convoy right ahead of us. Ed Ross used to say "Boy, red-dog is really on the loose." We'd be waiting for red-dog to catch us. It was tough on the crew. I noticed there would be an awful lot of people sleeping up on deck. See, the crew's quarters were below the waterline. People would move up and sleep on the deck. I guess it felt safer.

DuFau: I'll bet you can count on my fingers the number of nights I slept below deck when we were on convoy duty. I used to sleep up on the signal bay. I just didn't want to be below deck. Two-thirds of the crew were in after quarters. There were two sections down there, but you had only one hatch to come out of. From my compartment I had to go into another compartment to get to the ladder to come up topside. With that number of men coming single file out of that hole, that was too long for me. I was scared. So I just spent most of my time up on the bridge sleeping on the stack. I'd sleep in my clothes in a parka, and it was very warm. A lot of the clothing now was invented then. We had that thin lining inside and the layers that would stop the cold. We had a hood, like an aviator's cap, that you'd put over your head to keep your ears warm.

War Diary (15 July 1944): Patrolling as before on starboard bow of convoy CK-3 bound from Azores to United Kingdom ports. . . . At 1625 all hands at battle stations for false sound contact; no charges dropped. At 2312 green flare reported bearing 135°–no further indication of presence of other units.

Garrison: On our first trip we got a report from a bomber that there were three submarines surfaced about twenty miles from the convoy. The minute the word came down from the bridge that they were close to us, we expected to get a call to go to general quarters, to battle stations. We were anxious to go and get them. We were young and didn't know how dangerous it could be. I was twenty, and I guess I wanted to go get those guys. But we never got the order to go get them because the main idea of a DE in a convoy was not so much to attack the submarine but to get the ships we were taking over there intact. To get them over with the supplies that were needed. So we didn't attack the U-boats. That was disappointing.

We wanted to go. We were excited. We thought, "This is it!"

There were simpler dangers closer at hand. Just moving on the ship could cause injury.

Farrell: The *Mason* was a BDE—that means a British destroyer escort. She was intended to be supplied to the British, and then the U.S. Navy decided to keep her. On the BDE you couldn't go from forward to aft on the ship without going out on the main deck. You had to get out on the main deck in the wind and rain, with water breaking over the ship, to go down to where you wanted to be. It was dangerous because the ship used to roll pretty bad. You would have to run down across that wet deck. You'd think you could put your hand right in the water, and the next thing you knew you were up in the air. You had to hold onto a lifeline. It was a miserable thing.

DuFau: From the crew's quarters in the second and third section you had to travel topside to get up to the mess hall area and up to the bridge, up forward. But you had to go up on the boat deck that was higher than the main deck, and they had stanchions lined . . . you would hold on to both to travel back and forth. They would encourage you to travel at least in twos because of the danger of being washed overboard.

Graham: Going back and forth in all kinds of weather was second nature for a sailor. We didn't pay any special attention; we knew subconsciously just what to do. I remember one night when the lifeline on the starboard side was washed out, and I was coming from the radio shack. Generally, you would go forward on the starboard side and rear on the port side. But out on the sea you would use any side. I always used the starboard side. And I came by that night reaching for the line that wasn't there. All I had to do was stumble, and I'd have been in the water.

Just before they arrived it looked as if their training would pay off. What seemed to be a German plane appeared. If it was on reconnaissance, it might be radioing their position to the U-boats. This could be it.

War Diary (18 July 1944): Patrolling as before on starboard bow of convoy CK-3 bound from the Azores to United Kingdom ports. At 0350 unidentified plane showing navigation lights passed overhead on course about 320°. At 1350 assumed SA radar guard. At 1905 all hands at battle stations. Unidentified aircraft bearing 170°, range 35 miles. Aircraft maneuvered around; then proceeded on course 110 until radar contact was lost. Plane last heading for St. Nazaire, France, apparently a "snooper." All fuses on 3"/50 cal ready ammunition set to barrage settings. Ready 20 mm machine guns increased to four. At 2248 all hands at battle stations. SA radar contact bearing 230°, contact lost almost immediately–no friendly indications received.

After the Normandy invasion on D-Day, June 6, the Allied troops had been fighting their way to isolate the peninsula. The U-boats, equipped with snorkels that allowed them to stay below for extended periods, radioed weather reports to the German commanders.

Graham: I think we were off of France sometime during the invasion. We had a GQ because of the German airplane that came in. It wouldn't come but so close, and we were all ready to go. But it turned around and went away. It was probably a reconnaissance plane. We were close enough to France to actually hear the guns. It would give you time to think about it. You wouldn't hear just one gun, you'd hear "Boom! Boom!" reports from many guns. That was the only time I was nervous.

Farrell: I hated going to general quarters. It was a miserable situation. It was either a half hour or an hour before sunrise and a half hour or an hour before sunset. So you're laying in your bunk and you're sound asleep, and you hear this general alarm going off. First of all, you don't know what time it is and whether it really is a contact with a submarine. You have to hop out of a nice warm bed and get on a tin hat and a life jacket. Then you'd sit at your station for an hour or an hour and a half, whatever it be, until sunrise—and you'd have the same thing at night.

We had many contacts when we were under way. In the middle of the night, you'd just get the general alarm. And to this day, when I hear it on TV, I get a twinge in my stomach every time I hear the doggone thing.

Divers: When we went to general quarters, Captain Blackford took the conn. When he was on the bridge of the ship, during all of the trips we made on convoy, he was in complete charge. I was quartermaster, and I worked with the navigator, Lieutenant Ross. I used to have to take 12:00 o'clock position reports. Mr. Ross would make them up, and I would take them to the captain for his signature. I got to know him pretty well. When we went to general quarters, Captain Blackford knew exactly what to do. He was very much in charge, and everybody had a lot of confidence in him. It makes a hell of a lot of difference if you've got confidence in the people in charge. You don't worry. You can do your job. You can perform your duties better because you don't have that thought behind you that maybe the ship is going to sink. We had very deep confidence in Captain Blackford's leadership.

Graham: We'd try to decipher the German codes to see what was going on. But we knew there were German subs and that they were in the area with the convoy. We would have to go to general quarters if there was a contact. I loved going to battle stations! When that gong went off and went "Dong-Dong-Dong," I loved to hear that song. I still like to sing that—"Dong-Dong-Dong." You see, just for a split second, you'd say, "Oh, Lord, it's a sub." It was just thrilling to me, just thrilling. And I wanted it to be a sub! We wanted to put the insignia on the stack. You would paint a submarine with a torpedo in it going down if you made a kill. But some guys were deathly afraid. A guy in the radio shack threw up on the typewriter.

Garrison: The alarm for general quarters triggered an instantaneous response. You didn't think, "This is it," you just reacted. My life jacket was attached to the bunk over me. One hand went up to get it, your foot hit the deck, and in seconds you were on your way. I don't remember if, when the GQ alarm sounded, I had to put on shoes or something like that. I mean, it seemed to me that you were almost ready instantaneously.

Thomas Young witnessed GQ as a drama and tried to make his audience feel as if they were there.

Thomas W. Young: ABOARD THE USS MASON AT SEA—(Delayed)—The first General Quarters alarm was sounded our very first day at sea aboard this destroyer escort on its maiden combat voyage. This was the call to arms, the sobering warning that these Negro rated men and specialists were at last really in the war as part of Uncle Sam's fighting Navy.

Early that morning the *Mason* had put to sea from an Atlantic Coast port as one of the escorting vessels for a convoy of merchant ships bearing vital war goods to the fighting fronts. For weeks the crew had been conditioned and trained for this important job. Here, suddenly and dramatically, was the moment that would tell how well these men had prepared themselves for the test.

Any reasonably well-established contact with enemy aircraft, surface ships or submarines was sufficient to send every man aboard to his battle station.

The only threat that concerned the *Mason* crew this close to home shores was that of the U-boat. But our phenomenal detection devices were kept ever tuned to report the approach of any unseen enemy craft. And every warning—every reasonably certain warning—must be heeded. Naturally, you get some false alarms that way.

At "GQ"—that's short for general quarters—every man has a definite station, a particular job to do. When the alarm sounds he must get to his post as rapidly as possible.

Since there are virtually three complete crews aboard a warship like this—one for each four-hour watch during a twelve-hour period—some men must necessarily take GQ assignments different from the jobs they are trained for and which they perform regularly.

For instance, only three radio operators may be required at any one time, but working in shifts of four hours on duty and eight off, it requires nine operators to maintain uninterrupted radio service throughout the day.

So three are given permanent radio assignments for general quarters, but the other six are placed throughout the ship where their services may be most needed.

It all works out very well because for ordinary war cruising it is unnecessary to man all the guns. Yet when a fight is on, a full team is needed at every weapon.

That is how a lot of seamen and steward's mates and firemen became heroes. On a warship, when the call to arms is sounded every man aboard becomes a fighting man.

Others take posts as lookouts, or join damage control parties, or man the depth charges, or take stations along the ship's amazingly intricate telephone system so that orders can be speedily and effectively passed along to the crew and information from every quarter of the vessel can be funneled into one center for effective conning of the ship.

A GQ is a tense, exciting experience, no matter how many you've been through before. You may be sleeping, or eating, or playing cards or exchanging funny stories on the fantail. When the gong begins to ring and a voice on the public address system sternly orders, 'All hands, man your battle stations!'—well, you tingle just a little bit inside because you don't know then how far away the enemy is or in what strength he will strike.

The speed with which the entire crew gets to its various battle stations is little short of amazing. Everywhere men are snatching up steel helmets and life jackets—required to be worn by all hands during GQ—and dashing briskly to their posts.

Every possible detail is thought about and provided for. One detail must close and secure all portholes before taking stations as ammunition handlers or damage control men. Others must lock all hatches.

On the *Mason* I think I was the only person without a fixed station at GQ. As the only war correspondent aboard for this history-making voyage, I was determined to miss no single bit of action that might make a good story. Having the run of the ship, so to speak, I tried out a variety of places before settling on the one that gave me the best vantage point for witnessing whatever happened.

The war diary describes the spectacular phenomenon that marked the safe completion of the *Mason*'s maiden voyage.

War Diary (21 July 1944): Patrolling as before. 0205 entire mast and rigging enveloped in "Saint Elmo's fire." All radios faded out completely. 1250 landfall by SL radar on Rodgers Tr., Lands End England. 2000, convoy lying to 10 miles west of Trevose Head waiting clearance of outbound convoy. At 2321 convoy fair in swept channel. . . . Convoy in two columns, escorts running parallel course up and down the sides.

Buchanan: I was reading the log a couple of weeks ago, and I read this part about Saint Elmo's fire. That's something a lot of people haven't heard anything about. But in the record it says on July 21, 1944, at 0205, the entire mast and rigging was lit up with Saint Elmo's fire.

I was on the bridge that night, out on the flying bridge. It was, you know, two in the morning. And Lieutenant Philips was on watch at the same time I was. And all of a sudden, I saw all this light. There are guide wires that go up to the mast and go down the other side of the mast; they stabilize the mast and anchor it in. Where I was standing, the wires came right over my head. The whole wire looked like neon blue light. It was the most beautiful thing I had ever seen. And when I saw it and realized how much light was all around me, the first thing I thought was, "I'm in a convoy and there are submarines out there. What a message to them!" I couldn't *believe* this! It was so bright, but it was just so beautiful. I looked over to see if any other ships had it, but they were at least a half a mile or a mile away.

Lieutenant Phillips saw it. We were talking about it. Not many sailors have ever actually seen that. It's an electrical phenomenon at sea in storms. There was a storm, and it was blowing like crazy. Then it got very warm. The light came and at the same time the radio faded out completely. I'm not sure what causes it, but it's an amazing sight.

I was so happy to get my verification from the log because even aboard ship, the guys didn't see it, not everybody, only the fellows on the bridge.

Deck Log (24 July 1944): 04–08 Steaming as before. Commenced steering various courses conforming to channel. Navigator plotting on bridge. Captain has conn. 0606–All engines stopped. 0710–All engines ahead one-third. 0750–Moored in Bangor Harbor, Ireland. Ready to get underway on half hour's notice. War Cruising watch still on. . . . All divisions make preparations to get underway. 1530–All divisions ready to get underway. 1545–Set special sea details. 1549–Anchor aweigh and underway. Captain on conn, navigator on bridge standing up Lough Foyle for Belfast Harbor on orders from C.T.G. 27.5. 1621–Pilot R. W. CRAIG aboard. 1623–Changed speed to 12 knots. 1630–Pile light abeam to starboard. 1634–Entered channel to Belfast Harbor. Red cage buoy No. 2 abeam to Starboard.

War Diary (24 July 1944): Screening Clyde section of convoy CK-3 bound from Charleston, S.C., to United Kingdom ports in company with USS STERN (DE-187) C.T.G. 27.5 in "STERN". At 0300, parted company with convoy and proceeded to Belfast with STERN, on receipt of orders from C.T.G. 27.5. 0750–Arrived Belfast Lough, fueled and provisions taken, and reported necessary repairs to C.T.G. 27.5. Liberty granted to one half ship's company at 1830.

The *Mason* left her convoy in Plymouth and headed first for Bangor harbor in Northern Ireland and then to Belfast. The log says they steamed up the River Foyle, but the Foyle flows into Derry on the west coast, at least one hundred miles from Belfast. Belfast Loch led them into the harbor and their first liberty. While the Republic of Ireland was technically neutral during World War II, the north of Ireland, as part of the United Kingdom, had been at war since 1939. Belfast had suffered through a blitz in April 1941, and the evidence of bombs was everywhere. For the people of Northern Ireland the arrival of the Yanks was a joyful deliverance. For many of the GIs Ireland was a home away from home. Many had roots in counties north and south. The families of twelve American presidents emigrated from northern counties. There were many stories of family reunions, albeit families that had been separated by a hundred years. More than three hundred thousand U.S. servicemen and women passed through the north from 1942 to 1945, and they made an enormous impact on this small place whose population was under one million. As one woman said, "It was a wonderful, exciting time." But when the crew of the *Mason* stood on deck taking third-class liberty, that is, watching the shore through field glasses, they felt some trepidation.

DuFau: It was a question in our minds. What were we going to meet? How would the people greet us? Because here we were, so many black guys. There were 160 of us on our ship. Whenever we went ashore, the captain always told us, "Don't go alone. Stay together, no matter what." So, that was in our minds. But then these greetings started coming without any effort on our part. That was like another world to us because never in my life until that day had I been treated like that. Never in my life had we received such greetings from people, perfect strangers. It's hard to find words to describe the Belfast experience, what we felt to be received the way we were by the people. We actually had a lady apologize for the weather conditions. She was wishing it was a sunshiny day, because it was so beautiful there, and she wanted us to see it so beautiful. She was sorry it was overcast.

That was such a great time. We went into the parks, and everybody greeted us so well. It was just a wonderful, wonderful experience. We had to travel from our own home country, our own home town, over all this water, to get to a place where people treated us like human beings.

Peters: Ireland was a great place to go. It wasn't our first foreign port, because we had had our first shakedown in Bermuda. But Bermuda was a disappointment to me. Bermuda was predominantly black; it was British, but it was black. Even though it was a foreign country, I experienced the same kind of discrimination that I experienced in this country—I was barred from the USO down there because I was black. I had the same uniform, the same ratings and everything that the white sailors had, yet we were not allowed to frequent that USO.

When we went to Ireland, it was a completely different story. It was like being liberated. It was like being . . . being . . . How can I put it? It was something we had never experienced in this country in terms of, "You're welcome here and we love you." That's literally the way it was. And I really still have a soft spot in my heart for Ireland.

William Bland: All the boys on the *Mason* were raised right here in this country, in the United States, and we couldn't go to a movie show or sit down at a counter in Woolworth's even. We had to go around to the back. And the next thing you know, we were on the ship, and we were scared. Then we went to Ireland, and the Irish people didn't look on us as our skin color. They looked on us as Americans—as American fighting men.

Grant: One thing I remember is that the girls were beautiful, and they didn't wear any makeup. No makeup of any kind. Not one. We got invited to this dance, and they were doing these Irish dances. At first I couldn't get it, I couldn't get the beat. They'd go this way, and the band would change, and they'd go that way, and I couldn't follow. Then I listened and I got it. First we'd move right, then left . . . dah, dah, dah. It was beautiful.

Buchanan: There was a girl sitting with us at the dance, and she said to me, "Did you ever hear of the blackit?" And I heard that word black and my ears perked up. Was she sitting here calling me a black something?

"What did you say?" I said. And then I understood.

Radioman 2/c James W. Graham

Signalman 2/c Gordon D. Buchanan

Signalman 2/c Lorenzo A. DuFau

Quartermaster 2/c Charles W. Divers

Radioman 3/c Merwin A. Peters

Motor Machinist's Mate 3/c Albert Watkins

Radioman 3/c Benjamin G. Garrison

Sonarman 3/c Arnold Gordon

Yeoman 3/c Mel Grant

Radarman 3/c George Polk

Seaman 1/c William H. Bland III

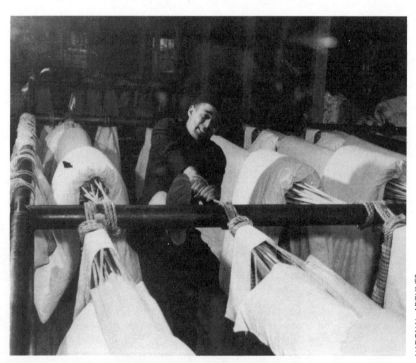

President Roosevelt's valet George C. Fields tightens hammocks in the barracks at Camp Robert Smalls.

Enlistees, including Gordon "Skinny" Buchanan, study semaphore at Great Lakes Naval Training Station, Illinois.

Entertainers at boot camp featured jazz greats like Dorothy Donegan, seen here performing with the Great Lakes Swing Band.

Some of the *Mason*'s future crew graduated from Camp Robert Smalls in 1943.

"Those guys were professionals," recalls Winfrey Roberts of the men he boxed at Great Lakes. Bill Leggett (*second from left*) also served on the *Mason*.

Wife of the inspiring prize-fighter Joe Louis, Marva Louis attended the graduation ceremonies at Camp Robert Smalls.

Gunnery mates receive specialized training at one of the navy's service schools.

James Graham (*right*) trains at the radio school of the Norfolk Naval Training Station.

Some of the *Mason*'s engineering crew studied at the Hampton (Virginia) Institute.

The African American Press reflected on what was regarded as the condescending and unfair nature of naval policy in early 1944.

The USS *Mason* was commissioned on 20 March 1944 at the Charlestown shipyard in Boston. Attending the ceremonies were (*left to right*): Capt. William M. Blackford, Lt. Comdr. Charles C. Pynne, the governor of Massachusetts, Leverett Saltonstall, and the city's mayor, Maurice J. Tobin, along with crew members.

The skipper whose crew would "follow him to hell and back," Captain
Blackford.

Breaking in to life on board ship, Signalman "Snafu" DuFau (*left*) assists "Chubby" Jones.

William Bland III handles the gun.

"Rip" Johnson was a member of the "black gang" in the *Mason*'s engine room.

A moment of relaxation: James Graham sits on the smoke generators on the fantail with buddy Radarman 2/c Kieffer.

Mason crewmen—eager to go ashore yet cooperative—pose for a shipmate.

By August 1944 the *Mason* was sporting Battle of the Atlantic camouflage, and her gunner's mates conducted regular drills on the "pom-pom" gun at sea.

Buchanan's skills at ship identification and his knowledge of German proved to be extremely beneficial to the *Mason* in her convoy duty.

Even the calmer moments while escorting convoy NY-119 were filled with worry about the unseaworthy yard tugs.

Marine artist Carl Evers's "The Ordeal of Convoy NY-119" depicts the tempest that threatened to swallow up the tugs and their escorts.

The two remarkable crewmen who kept their cool under record-breaking winds and waves to weld the broken *Mason* en route to safety.

Arnold Gordon (center) clowns around with shipmates while on liberty in Oran, Algeria, in the early months of 1945. Winfrey Roberts, (*top right*) an electrician's mate third class, likewise savors the exotic liberty in Oran.

At war's end, the *Mason* saw a change of command. Capt. Norman Meyer took over for Captain Blackford (*below*—seen congratulating the new skipper), who was promoted and transferred to Great Lakes.

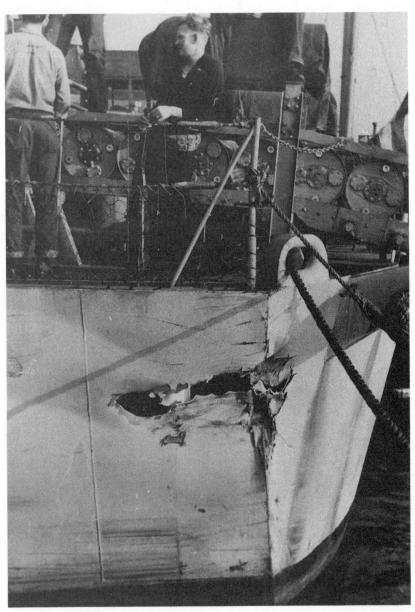

Under Captain Meyer's direction shortly after he came aboard, the *Mason* rammed the USS *Spangenburg* (DE 223) while pulling into a North River pier in New York City. (*Facing page*) The skipper and "Nuckles" Covington assess the damage.

Lt. (j.g.) James Hair was recruited both for his ship-handling ability and his black heritage.

The U.S. Coast Guard inducted black sailors to patrol American beaches. The crew of the *Mason* encountered them in New Jersey and the New England states.

Gaining the official recognition the *Mason*'s crewmen so rightly deserve, Lorenzo DuFau (*left*) and James Graham (*center*) celebrate in Annapolis with Admiral Kelso, former chief of naval operations, and Admiral Lynch, former Naval Academy superintendent.

After the "Passing of the Colors," Brigade Commander Jeff Royal and his parents are congratulated by DuFau and Graham.

Newlyweds James and Barbara Graham join Charles Divers and friend for some liberty at the Mandalay Club in Harlem. (*Top*) The picture of Gordon Buchanan's sister, "Sweet Bobbie," that inspired a fifty-year love match.

President Clinton honors the men of the *Mason* with a certificate of appreciation that states, "A grateful nation remembers your sacrifices and contributions during World War II."

Celebrating the fiftieth anniversary of the *Mason*'s commissioning are (*clockwise from bottom left*): Gordon Buchanan, James Graham, Lorenzo DuFau, Barbara Graham, Ruby Grant, Mary Pat Kelly, Mel Grant, Albert Watkins, Charles Divers, Terry DuFau, Uldine Garrison, Benjamin Garrison, and Mansel Blackford.

"Did you ever hear of the black out?" she repeated.

"Oh, sure," I said. "We have them in New York all the time."

Garrison: There was a girl sitting on one side of me and a shipmate was sitting on the other side. I had never learned to dance, but everybody was dancing, so somebody came up and asked this girl to dance. She turned to me and asked, "May I dance with him?" Now that made an impression on me. It showed me how courteous she was, how courteous all of the people were. And I still remember her name—Sadie O'Neill. I'll never forget it.

The Irish people were very friendly, very cordial, very polite, very courteous. The only problem we had was that we didn't stay there long enough. We stayed in Belfast about one night. Actually, I think the reason we didn't stay any longer was because a report got back to the ship about how well we were treated, and some of the white boys couldn't take that. And so they took us the next day up to Londonderry, and there they dropped anchor. We didn't go ashore in Londonderry, but we did go ashore in Belfast and had a wonderful time.

DuFau: It was such a shock to be treated so well, especially when we compared it to our own United States Navy.

Garrison: When we talk about Ireland and how well we were received, you might get the idea that it was a novelty for them. But there had been black soldiers there, so our coming was not a novel experience. It was just their normal way of treating people.

Watkins: We enjoyed Ireland very much. There were about four of us, and we bought papers from a little fellow who took us on a tour of Belfast. At the end, we said, "Well, let's go in so we can have a beer." So we all waited while the barman pulled this big stopper and handed us these great big pints of beer. We all drank it down together, and we spit it out on the floor! They just cracked up. They said, "We have nothing but warm beer." Yech!

But I must say, we enjoyed Ireland. People were nice to us; they were very nice. It was something we weren't quite used to.

Bland: In other places they called us "Tan Yankees," but in Ireland, they called us "Yanks," the same thing they called the white sailors. "Yanks." And it was good.

But the interlude in Ireland was short and the *Mason* soon took on, appropriately enough, 4,032 pounds of potatoes and 336 pounds of cabbage and prepared to leave Belfast. A local pilot, H. C. Reddy, guided them out into the channel. They increased speed to seventeen knots and set out for New York. But their reception in Ireland had a profound effect on the men. Thomas Young devoted a whole article to the experience. He titled it, "Irish First to Treat Mason Crew as Americans."

Young: ABOARD THE USS MASON AT SEA—(Delayed)—If the USS *Mason* ever goes AWOL it's a fairly safe bet that the search planes will locate it promptly by flying over a certain port in Northern Ireland. For, although the world-traveling men on this destroyer escort with a predominantly Negro crew may see a great many famous and fabulous places, there is one little spot on the Irish Sea that will always hold a top place in their esteem. That city is one to which the *Mason* paid a brief visit after helping to deliver a convoy of vital war goods to ports in the British Isles. 'Why, we're not citizens of New York or Chicago or Atlanta or even of just the United States,' one of the seamen said reflectively the day after we left Ireland. 'We're citizens of the world.' His was the mood prevailing throughout the ship. 'Funny,' he mused, 'how I had to come all the way across the ocean to a foreign country before I got to enjoy the feeling of being an American.'

The difference was people, just plain people—the way those people treated them during their two-day visit. The hospitality they enjoyed was not the kind shown strangers the first time and then put aside. The Irish had seen the Americans in their midst for years, hundreds of thousands of them—soldiers, sailors, fliers. Many of the soldiers stationed so long in Northern Ireland were colored so the sight of the *Mason* crew was not new either. One-half of the men were given liberty in town the first night and the other half the second night. They walked the streets, frequented the pubs (where nothing more potent than traditional luke-warm beer was available) and stores.

But after almost six weeks on the sea more than half the men spent their evenings at dance halls where a large group of friendly local girls helped to bring back memories of home, of parties and laughter and sweethearts. When the dance was over many of them escorted the girls home. One of the lads expressed it oddly, but I suspect he had the thought of all the rest in mind when he said, 'It was the first time in my life that I've been treated like a real American.'

We are now racing across the Atlantic again in the endless pursuit of German U-boats, and memories of that last night in Ireland are fresh. Several of the men have asked me how I liked the place. It had been disappointing. It wasn't in the class with Casablanca, Algiers, London or Liverpool. So I am being as honest as blunt when I sum up my experience there as 'lousy.' Invariably, a sly grin comes across their faces as they look at me out of the corner of their eyes. 'That's funny,' they remark, thoroughly suspicious of my veracity; 'everybody else had a swell time.' Then they recite some of the interesting and exciting details. By now, I am completely persuaded that the men of the *USS Mason* enjoyed one of the great moments of their lives during the visit to Ireland. It was the people of that Northern Irish seaport who gave them that moment.

Deck Log (28 July 1944): 00–04 At passage from Belfast, N. Ireland to New York, U.S.A. with C.T.G. 27.5 in compliance with orders to this group. Base course 249 degrees True. Standard speed set at 15 knots. . . . Steaming in line of bearing formation at 3,000 yards distance to the guide and steering various courses and setting various speeds to keep on proper station. Four main engines in use. Continuous search being made on the SL radar* searching on the four-mile scale for four minutes and on the ten-mile scale for one minute. SA radar** in a standby condition. Sound gear in continuous search from 70 degrees on either beam forward. No. 2 3"/50 1.10/75 and two (2) MM guns in ready condition and antisubmarine armament manned.

War Diary (28 July 1944): Steaming as before. Course 249 degrees, speed 17 knots. At 0820, changed course to 251 degrees. At 1322, all hands at battle stations. STERN appeared to have good sonar contact. All ships maneuvered in box formation five (5) miles from contact point. At 1930, secured from battle stations, and rejoined formation with other ships. All ships proceeded en route as before. At 1700, set clocks to Plus 30 minutes zone time. 2200

---

* AS = band surface radar, with a thirteen-mile range, having been developed in the early 1940s.
** The "bed-spring" type radar screen on the foremast, used for air searches. Built by RCA, it was a DE's primary air-search radar.

to 2305, zigzagging according to plan No. 8 F.T.P. 2304–
Formation course changed to 243 degrees True.

These log and war diary excerpts reflect a change in the *Mason*'s
mission. Rather than shepherding a convoy back home, the ship
had joined with other DEs to form a hunter/killer group. Their
assignment was to pursue and, if possible, to capture a U-boat, or
else sink it. The USS *Pillsbury*, a DE that was part of such a group,
had been instrumental in the capture of the U-505 and even now
was towing it back to Bermuda. This would be the first naval prize
taken at sea by the United States since the War of 1812. If the *Mason*
could capture or sink a U-boat, the men could finally paint the prized
emblem on their stack.

Young: With the war against the deadly submarine menace in the
Atlantic swiftly coming to a close, it becomes increasingly
difficult for the hunters of these underseas raiders to locate and
destroy their prey. On the trip across no U-boat attacked our
convoy or challenged the might of the escort warships bristling
with anti-submarine weapons and armament. After the relatively
slow and sometimes tedious trip eastward at the end of which
we delivered our cargo ships without loss, most of the men were
genuinely disappointed because they had not had a chance to
strike a real blow at the enemy, or to match their courage and
skill against that of the Nazi raiders. Then came one of the
greatest thrills of the entire trip when we learned that our task
force, consisting entirely of destroyer escorts, was to return to
the United States, without a convoy, as a 'killer group.' This time
we were to go off the defensive and take the offensive. We were
going out looking for the enemy, to find him and destroy him.

This was something new. The tactics of an escort group with
a convoy to deliver is to get the ships to the other side, avoiding
submarines if possible and fighting them only when they bring
the fight to you. But now we were the hunters and the U-boats
were the hunted. How well would we be able to fight them when
we tracked them down? As this fleet of DEs headed westward
across the North Atlantic, executing maneuvers and formations
throughout the day and night, we all experienced that feeling
of tense expectancy which usually precedes a great dramatic
moment. How did the *Mason* crew face this uncertain destiny

during the hours and days of suspense as they waited for lightning to strike? What kind of fighting sailors do these Negro bluejackets make? How well do they master the intricate technical devices and scientific machinery used in anti-submarine warfare?

Farrell: There were a lot of anti-black stereotypes going around. That they wouldn't be able to run the ship maybe! There were even people saying, "Oh, gee, they'll get out there, and the first time a gun gets shot off, they're going to be so scared they will be jumping overboard! All the officers will have to bring it (the ship) back." That kind of weird stuff. I can tell you this, when the guns were going off, there was no difference between black and white.

Deck Log (28 July 1944): 12–16 Steaming as before. 1243–Daily inspection of magazine temperature and smokeless powder samples made. Conditions normal. Sprinkling system tested satisfactory. . . . 1321–Changed speed to standard. Sounded general alarm for all hands to man battle stations as *USS STERN* was flying submarine attack flag. 1325–Condition "Able" reported set throughout the ship. Ordered to join other ships on course 000 degrees True, and zig zag. . . . 1355–Secured from General Quarters. 1425–Manned battle stations. Went into box search around area with *USS POWERS* acting as head of our section of three ships. Captain has conn.

Although there were close calls, depth charges were dropped, and K-guns were shot, no submarines were captured or sunk. But the crew had proven their ability both as shepherds and hunters. And on a private level, an event that would affect the *Mason*'s history had already taken place.

Graham: One morning I was coming off duty, and Skinny Buchanan had his sister Barb's picture on his bunk, writing a letter. I saw it and said, "Who is that?"

"That's my sister."

"It is?"

"Yes."

"Do you mind if I write her a letter?"

He said, "No." So I wrote her a letter.

Buchanan: One day my future brother-in-law saw my sister's picture as I was writing her a letter, and he fell in love with the picture. He asked me if he could write to my sister, and I said, "Yes!" You know, it was no big deal. We were all sailors together, no problem. But that kind of started and kept up without my knowing it. Eventually, Graham came to my home and met my sister.

War Diary (2 September 1944): 0909–Moored berth Number Two (2), Navy Yard, New York for eight days availability in accordance with instructions from FAO, New York.

Graham: As soon as we reached port in New York—it must have been about nine o'clock—Skinny and I got off the ship lickety-split. We went to Jamaica (Long Island), where his family was living. I was more anxious to get to his house than he was, and his sister Barbara was not at home! His mother put me in the guest room to sleep, and I woke up to find Barb tucking in the blankets at the foot of the bed. I looked at her, and the first thing I said was, "I'm going to marry you some day." And I did.

The *Mason*'s first voyage was over—a success in every way. Thomas Young reported "not a single unpleasant moment" during the entire seven weeks.

Young (letter to the director of public relations, Navy Department): I am happy to say that the entire experience with the USS Mason was a most enlightening and pleasant one. The cheerful cooperation extended to me by everyone aboard, from the Commanding Officer down to the lowest rated seaman, was gratifying. During the entire seven weeks that I was living among these men there was not a single unpleasant moment that I know of.

The crew of the Mason wants to make good, and, from my observations it is entirely capable of doing so. One fortunate circumstance, it seems to me, is the further fact that they have a thoroughly competent Commanding Officer who has won both the confidence and admiration of the men.

For the privilege of going out with the Mason on its first combat assignment I am deeply grateful to the officials of the Office of Public Relations who approved my request.

Convoy NY-119

The task group commander called it "The Battle of the Barges," or "Men and Barges against the Sea" in his formal report to Atlantic command of the U.S. Navy. In describing convoy NY-119, in which four DEs escorted a convoy of army tugs and barges from New York to Portsmouth, England, Comdr. Alfred L. Lind's emotions push dry official language aside, and something of the drama of this ill-fated convoy is conveyed.

First, he states the facts. The men in his command had fought the sea for "thirty days and three hours." They had traveled "3,539 miles at an average speed of 4.74 miles per hour." During the first twenty days they faced ten-foot seas and twenty-mile-per-hour winds—difficult but normal for the North Atlantic in October. If that weather had held, the convoy would have crossed with few losses, and Commander Lind's report would have been brief and matter-of-fact. "However, from October 10 to 23rd, inclusive, the wind persisted without abating from twenty to forty-two miles per hour with gusts reported to ninety miles per hour, and the seas built up to forty to fifty feet, with an average of twenty-three feet for the fourteen-day period." This, he said, was "The Battle of the Barges."

The barges were formidable indeed. Adm. Eugene Moran of the Moran Tugboat Company suggested that the barges used to ferry railroad cars across New York harbor would make excellent temporary piers in France. These heavily timbered floats were 250 to 360 feet long and 45 feet wide. Each one could carry ten to twelve railcars in two columns. They were designed to be tugged, alongside, across New York harbor, for about half an hour. Even then, as present-day tugboat captain George Matteson reports, they were extremely difficult to tow. "If you have to tow them behind on a hawser, they sometimes flip around, and the stern can be ahead of you. They are wild as hell. And heavy! They are full of iron—30 percent iron—and almost unsinkable because they are built with twelve compartments. To think of towing those monsters across the ocean, it's amazing anybody got out of that convoy alive."

In the crucible of wind, waves, and wooden monsters, men lost their lives and vessels faltered. The storm sank three tugs, eight steel car floats, and five wooden cargo barges. Nineteen men were lost. Lind said in his report that many more craft and lives would have been lost if he had not detached the small craft from the barges and sent them ahead. The ship chosen to shepherd this detachment into port was the *Mason*. In a sense this would be the crew's finest hour. Not only did the *Mason* guard the ships in her charge as they pushed against the wind and sea, but with land in sight and no charts available, the crew led them from buoy to buoy through a treacherous channel to safety. Then, taking only two hours to weld fast her cracked deck, the *Mason* went back to sea to assist the stranded convoy.

Commander Lind recommended that each man in the crew of the *Mason* receive a letter of commendation. They never did. Yet the story of NY-119 could not be told without mentioning the *Mason*. When Charles Dana Gibson wrote "The Ordeal of Convoy 119" in 1973, he interviewed crew members of the *Mason*. But even Gibson, who quotes from Lind's report, does not mention that the commander recommended individual commendations.

NY-119 began forming in New York harbor in late August 1944. The invasion of France was well under way. Supplying the troops and rebuilding bombed-out ports, roads, and bridges became an urgent priority. The Allies pushed toward Germany. The U-boats were equipped now with snorkels and radar-intercept gear that allowed them to evade air patrols and concentrate on selected targets as they prepared for the final push of late winter 1944. During the time the ships of convoy NY-119 were gathering in New York harbor, *U-482* sank a British corvette, the U.S. tanker *Jacksonville*, and three other merchant ships just fifty miles from Derry, Northern Ireland. Closer to home, the hurricane was in full swing and the convoy waited in port for more moderate weather. Men would die and ships would sink because of that delay. But as the men of the *Mason* waited to set out, they had no sense of disaster ahead. The wait meant more liberty, more nights at Small's Paradise or the Club De Lys.

War Diary (11–18 September 1944, inclusive): Moored 33rd Street Pier, South Brooklyn, New York, receiving provisions, training, etc., and making special preparation for escorting a transatlantic convoy of Army Tugs and barges, accompanied by other small craft. Received the following despatches relating to organization of convoy NY-119 and escort: (a) *Cinclant's Secret Despatch 221503* of *August* forming Task Group 27.5 with ComCortDiv. 80 as C.T.G. Group consisting of USS MAUMEE (AO-2), USS ABNAKI (AT-96), USS O'TOOLE (DE-527)–(Flag), POWERS (DE-528), BERMINGHAM (DE-530), CHASE (DE-16); (b) *C.T.G. 27.5's Secret 181447* of *September,* indicating sailing date.

War Diary (11 September 1944): Verbal instructions received from ComCortDiv 80 to inspect and aid in training personnel of convoy prior to sailing. Inspections showed majority of personnel involved to be extremely inexperienced. Original sailing date delayed because of tropical hurricane.

Graham: We weren't informed officially of the reasons for the delay, but in the radio shack we got the messages and we passed them on. They wouldn't tell us anything as a crew, but we would get the information. Say, if a weather report came in that was significant to us in the radio shack, we would just type it out and let it follow the usual routine of going to the captain and the different officers after it was decoded. But, really, what we were doing and who we were going with was immaterial to us. All we wanted to know was whether or not we were going to England. We had never been there before. We would have a lot of fun. As far as whether, say, twenty ships, tugs, or this and that were going, it wasn't important to us, I don't think. Not to me, it wasn't, because I really didn't care one way or the other. We didn't know the significance of the convoy.

DuFau: Scuttlebutt got around. We found out that the convoy was made up of tugboats and small coastal vessels. Some of the tugboats had to pull barges. Those tugboats and barges were to be used to rebuild Normandy harbor and make temporary piers after the invasion.

Divers: We had escorted all kinds of convoys. Some had troop ships, others had merchant marine ships and tankers. Our job was to deliver them, get them over there, which we did. We never lost a single ship except in convoy NY-119. We lost some ships and some men in the largest storm in the North Atlantic in the century.

Garrison: These tugboats were harbor tugs, and in my view they should never have been sent on a convoy like that. They were just frail and not seaworthy, and the crews weren't really prepared.

DuFau: As far as the crews of the tugs and the merchant ships, whether they were experienced or not, we never had any knowledge of that at all. We weren't in a position to even *judge* who had experience and who didn't have experience because we were green sailors ourselves.

Graham: We were going so slow, we could see the mainland for about five days. We were doing about five knots. And we didn't know anything about the weather or where we were going. We didn't even know that it was NY-119. Actually, the crew wouldn't know where we were going until maybe we were out in the ocean someplace, and a radioman would tell somebody. DuFau and Buchanan, as signalmen, might communicate with another ship and ask them questions. Then the guys would come around to the signalman or the radioman and ask them where we were going. They were anxious to know where we were going, but they didn't worry much about how many ships were in the convoy or anything like that. I know I didn't want to know anything like that.

DuFau: Those of us who had access to the chart that was laid out could go in and out of that chart room, and you could see the layout of the course. And we could do a lot of guesswork. It became scuttlebutt among the crew. You'd pick up little hints here and there. The officers would be talking, and you'd overhear bits and pieces. Then, when we were down below decks, we could put these things together. That's the way we could get a good idea of what way we were heading.

Garrison: We always felt that every convoy we were escorting was important and that we had to get it there safely. We knew that if a submarine fired a torpedo at, say, a carrier or an oiler or a ship in the convoy that was carrying cargo that just really had to get there, the escort commander could tell a destroyer escort to get between that ship and the torpedo. He could tell us to take the hit ourselves. We had fewer men, we were a smaller ship, and it was important that the larger ships survive. That's part of the game.

DuFau: You could hardly imagine that a convoy would travel as slow as we did on NY-119. You could only make the speed that the slowest ship could make.

Graham: There was a foreign captain of one of those tugs, and he just refused to lag behind or stay with the convoy. He wanted to go ahead, go ahead. The commodore, I think, was Admiral Lynn [Lind], and I think he gave Blackford orders to go up and see what was wrong with him. Blackford went back to see what was wrong, and he gave him a lot of baloney about this was wrong and that was wrong, and something like that. At that time there was an American sailor on board as a signalman, and he sent a message that said, "It's a goddamn lie," or something like that, so the commodore said, "Fire a volley over the bow of the ship." I think he told him in no uncertain terms that if he didn't keep up, "We'll blow you out of the water; you can't do this." They had no more trouble out of him.

War Diary (24 September 1944): Underway as before with convoy NY-119 bound for United Kingdom ports. At 0800 changed to screen on starboard bow of convoy. Wind and sea building up from N.E. Ceased patrolling sector at 2345. Some vessels of convoy doing poorly under existing conditions. LT-492 continually pulling ahead of station and straining her tow unnecessarily.

War Diary (25 September 1944): Changed position to forward picket at 0608. All preparations made for heavy weather. . . . Making considerable leeway.

Garrison: In the North Atlantic, when water hits the deck, the steel deck, it turns to ice immediately. That's how cold it is. And the ropes; we called them lines. If a line was two inches thick, by the time the ice hit it, it got four times as big and, of course, was difficult to handle. The decks are very slippery too. You can't walk upright. You have to time it. The ship is rolling and pitching and going up and down, and you have to time it. If you fall overboard, you're finished. You couldn't survive. The handrails were only waist high. If the deck was slanting and you lost your balance, you were gone. That's why the captain ordered that when you came topside, you had to have your life jacket on. Mandatory. You must. No question. It's rough, it's dark. Total darkness. It's slippery. The ship is bucking up and down, right and left. And you really have to time your movements. You cannot walk erect. Sometimes you'd have to actually stop and think about what you were going to do next because if you didn't, you were over the side.

Don't forget, aside from the *Maumee*, the DEs were about the largest vessels in the convoy, and when the storm started tossing *us* around, we could just imagine what it was doing to those tugs. Another indication of how rough it was, was the stragglers. A straggler is one who can't keep up with the convoy for some reason or another—maybe engine trouble or mechanical trouble or something. And the convoy commander would assign an escort to stay with the straggler if he could fix what was wrong. I know many times we'd hear them say, "Well, old boy, I'll see you. Sorry,"—and that's the last we saw of him. We didn't know what happened to him.

War Diary (26 September 1944): Patrolling as before. At 0217 distress call received from "ST-719"* who had capsized, while in tow of "LT-492".** POWERS, BERMINGHAM, and ABNAKI proceeded to pick up survivors, saving all but a few men. MASON returned to convoy to screen port bow. Convoy speed reduced to steerage way only. Wind force 5 at time ST-719 capsized. 1038–Convoy sufficiently reformed to increase speed to 4 knots. . . . Gyro still erratic. Convoy averaging 10 degrees leeway.

DuFau: In the radio shack we had TBS communication—ship to ship or ship to shore—but it was short-range. They had one up in the flying bridge with the captain, and you could hear him talking on the bridge, you could hear talking over to the other immediate ships. They were discussing the ship that capsized. We weren't allowed to turn on the searchlights or anything like that. Over the TBS I heard the voices say that they heard the screaming, the yelling in the background. I think that the *O'Toole* was assigned to pick up a lot of guys, because she was the flagship. We couldn't stop in the storm; we couldn't turn on any lights. We had to maintain our speed. One ship was actually close to rescuing one of the fellows who was overboard, but a wave drew him away and slammed him into the side of the ship at the time they were trying to rescue him and cracked his head open.

* S.T. = Army Small Tug, harbor tug
** L.T. = Army Large Tug, seagoing tug

Comdr. Alfred Lind (report): The first eighteen days at sea produced no unexpected casualties except the loss of the ST-719 which, except for the resultant loss of two lives, was not considered to be serious. Further, in that the immediate cause of its rolling over can not be attributed even to the bad weather but rather to its inherent instability, this incident can not be classed as unexpected. However, the storm of 25–26 September started 50 percent of the BCF steel car floats leaking and perhaps contributed largely to their ultimate loss through slowing down the entire convoy enough to lose at least two days in arrival at our ultimate destination. This proved to be about the margin between arriving safely and being completely broken up within 60 to 150 miles of FALMOUTH. The three obsolete and misfit Y-Oilers,* No. 126, 127 and 128, had also been a constant source of trouble, having occupied the services of two of the three service tugs about 70 percent of the time and also largely contributed to the slowing down of the convoy.

Garrison: In the New York-119 convoy, we lost quite a few men because the little tugboats we were towing over capsized. One of the destroyer escorts, in an attempt to rescue some men, crushed them. You just can't survive in that cold water. I mean, you're finished. Finished. A destroyer escort is about twelve feet wide at its widest. It's very small. It doesn't take much water. It sits up high on the water. It can make very steep turns, and it's fast—as fast as a submarine. DEs are very light and just bounce around like a wild horse, up and down, up and down. When you are sitting in the radio shack, the chair legs are in pipes welded to the deck. So, as the ship comes up, the equipment comes up into your face. When we were in a storm for two or three days, I couldn't change clothes, I couldn't eat because they couldn't keep food in the galley. That's the way it goes.

Watkins: I had been seasick all the way through the first voyage. We came back through the North Sea and all of that jumping up and down. On the second voyage, I was the oil king, and they were giving me more work, but I was still really sick. Someone came down and said, "Oh, you should go up and see the big waves." I was hesitant about going up there! But when I got up,

* Army harbor tankers

I saw the big waves, and I was so excited that I just stopped being seasick.

Divers: Captain Blackford took all that in stride because he was no amateur. He was a skipper before he came to the *Mason*. He was in the Aleutians, and he had skippered ships there, see. And that's some of the most terrible weather year-round. He was used to rough weather. To him it wasn't anything new.

Farrell: He [Blackford] loved it when it got rough! Now, there's nothing worse than a DE that's in rough weather. It almost stands up on its end. But he used to come down to the wardroom, and say, "You know, the rougher it gets, the better I like it."

It took us thirty-two days to go across. Of course, we didn't have enough oil to go that long, so we had to refuel at sea. It's rough, everyone's nervous, and you have to get this big line across from the tanker and take the oil on. That oil king better be on his toes, because the vents from the tanks are in the crew's sleeping quarters, and if he doesn't get it switched to another tank fast enough, that oil all comes up into the crew's sleeping quarters. Their lockers are on the deck, so everyone's clothing and their girlfriend's picture and everything else would be soaked in diesel oil. The oil king had an important job, but all the crew had to be good because it was tricky, very tricky, especially if the sea was rough or the weather bad.

War Diary (29 September 1944): Patrolling as before on starboard bow of convoy. At 0628 all escorts exercised anti-aircraft screening formation. AT 0700 MAUMEE left convoy to fuel escorts. MASON fuel to capacity at 1303. MAUMEE returned to convoy at 2200. . . . MASON assumed forward picket station after returning with MAUMEE.

Garrison: I've often thought, what would have happened had they sunk the *Maumee*?

Graham: We would have been up the creek.

DuFau: The whole convoy would have been messed up.

Garrison: One ship capable of refueling us. *One!* And if the Germans had sunk that one ship . . . Suppose they had sunk it around the Azores, because the Azores are about halfway across. Now, you have just as much distance to come back home as you do to go across.

Graham: We wouldn't have been able to move! We would have been stuck.

DuFau: We would have been sitting ducks.

Graham: And even if we had had enough fuel, you couldn't leave the convoy. You couldn't desert the others. You had to stay on station, stay with the convoy.

War Diary (30 September 1944): Patrolling as before. At 0630 commenced sweep to flank and took station on port bow of convoy. At 1105 took station astern of convoy with MAUMEE while she fueled small craft. At 1300 all ships back in normal position. All escorts streamed FXR* gear at 2300 upon receiving sonar contact report from forward picket. Contact false.

DuFau: Every time we got a contact there were all these changes to go through, decisions to make. The officer on the conn had to use his judgment to give commands to the quartermaster on the wheel—whoever was on the wheel—what way to steer. He had to try to take advantage of the ocean to stay as upright as possible. Several times we were thrown over pretty bad.

The officers would change, but we all knew that Captain Blackford was in charge. His skill would direct us on how to steer the ship and the speed, which helped us stay afloat without being zapped by the waves. We had confidence in our skipper, but we knew that ultimately we were at the mercy of The Man above.

The officer would give orders, but they depended on *men* doing their job. Everyone had his station to cover.

Farrell: Every man was important. The crew ran the engine room. If you broke something, you'd be out of commission. So you had to fix it while you were running, no matter what the weather or condition. You had to maintain your station in the convoy and make repairs and get it going again.

There was a lot of real complex equipment in that engine room that very few of us knew anything about a year previous to that. The crew had some training. The motor machinist's mates had gone to diesel school, the electrician's mates had gone to electrician's school, etc. Some members of the crew had gone to gyro school. As the engineering officer, I had some training, and I was by profession an electrical engineer, so I had some basis of knowledge of how a thing worked. The crew would have

---

* Foxer Gear was a noisemaking device towed to confuse torpedoes guided by acoustical devices.

to knock it down and repair it and get it back together, and believe me, in that convoy NY-119 we needed every bit of skill that we had.

At the beginning, more of the first-class mates in the engine room were white, though we did have some black first class. But we concentrated on going up the line. As soon as we could, we would qualify blacks who were second class and so forth as first class, and we'd qualify the first class as chiefs. As we did that, we would transfer the whites off the ship. When we took the ship out of commission, I don't think there were any white chiefs or first-class rates on the ship.

Peters: Convoy 119 was an interesting voyage, and it was a scary one. But we were kids; it was an adventure for me. Here we were in bad seas, in hurricane weather for thirty-one days. We were looking at seas that were forty to fifty feet high. We had to constantly run in circles, which is what you did when you were on convoy duty, shepherding the other ships.

I never really thought of the danger that was there. I guess as a kid I thought I was invincible, that I wasn't vulnerable to death.

The weather moderated as they reached the Azores, and there was some hope that the worst was over. Instead, it was yet to come.

Lind (report): When the weather again turned to storm proportions on 10 October the demand for service tugs increased in alarming rapidity, and when BCF 3203 again filled with water and turned over, it was quickly decided to sink her and destroy the wooden barge.

War Diary (12 October 1944): Screening as before in company with other escorts of CortDiv 80. At 0740 went astern of convoy to assist the other two escorts in that area, rounding up stragglers. At this time, POWERS and ABNAKI feel far enough astern with their stragglers to constitute a new section of the convoy. Resumed screening station at 0830. . . . Convoy having great difficulty in maintaining proper formation. Convoy averaging 15 degrees leeway. It will be impossible to pass through routed positions at this rate.

War Diary (13 October 1944): Screening as before. At 0406 left station to aid HMS ASTRAVEL with steering casualty. At 0927, rejoined screen as stern picket. At 1353 LT-63 reported one of her barges had capsized. MASON and O'TOOLE proceeded to sink same by gunfire. Wooden barge on top remained as a menace to navigation despite repeated effort to demolish it by gunfire and depth charges. Sea too high to risk putting a man on board with demolition charge.—20 MM incendiary ammunition started small fires that were immediately extinguished by seas and rain. . . . All other stragglers able to proceed without additional assistance. . . . Making 10 degrees leeway. Wind 15–28 knots westerly. Will be unable to follow scheduled route. Will pass 120 miles south of point "K."

Graham: Everybody was at his battle station. I was supervising the radio shack. I heard the guns and opened the hatch. I saw the shots skip off! Sooner or later, they gave it up. That was the *Mason* and the *O'Toole*. We were hitting the barge, but it was made out of wood, and we didn't make enough holes in it to allow water in to sink it. We had machine guns and everything on it. The gunnery was good, but the barge just wouldn't sink.

The convoy commander sent a message by semaphore to the *Mason*. The signalmen recorded it, and the information became scuttlebutt.

> DUE TO THE STRESS AND STRAIN OF EVENT YESTERDAY I MAY HAVE FORGOTTEN TO GIVE YOU AND YOUR EXCELLENT GUNNERS A WELL DESERVED "WELL DONE" FOR THEIR EFFECTIVE SHOOTING AAA THE MASON HAS PERFORMED EACH TASK ASSIGNED IN A MOST COMMEND-ABLE MANNER AAA PLEASE CONVEY MY APPRECIATION TO YOUR EXCELLENT CREW

War Diary (16 October 1944): Screening starboard bow as before. Wind and sea rising. Many breakdowns reported by small craft and increasing difficulty with tow wires. Some alarm noted in TBS transmission. Consoling words and helpful suggestions by Task Group Commander on T.B.S. did much to quiet them. Wind velocity about 40 knots. 0700–Convoy slowed to steerageway with many tows completely stopped. MAUMEE and the oilers back to pull ahead of the convoy to maintain steerageway. At 1718, Task Group Commander ordered MASON to form a new section of the convoy to keep the faster vessels (5 knots) from becoming scattered. This section had HMS PRETEXT appointed as commodore. All oilers, independent tugs plus HMS ASTRAVEL and PRETEXT pulled out to the left and proceeded ahead of convoy—drawing away slowly. . . . No sights obtainable after 0700. PRETEXT doing an excellent job in organizing ships into a passable sort of formation—aided greatly by her Radar and free use of T.B.S. radio. Considerable leeway indicates more bad weather coming. Section proceeding at 4 knots. Wind decreased to about 18 knots. Barometer still low.

Peters: Each day was a new day, each day was a new adventure. Personally, it was *the* great event, I guess you would call it. Thirty-one days out there in the middle of the ocean. But in some respects, it was tragic. Ships were lost. Lives of people were lost. We would discuss these things at chow; each night we'd talk about what ships went down and how many people had been lost. We were wondering if the next day was going to bring the same kind of thing.

But at that age you think you're going to live forever and you can survive anything that comes along. And that's pretty much the way I think most of the people aboard that ship felt. I never saw anybody really fearful that the ship was going to sink or that some bad thing was going to happen to us—although it was happening all around us. We had great confidence in ourselves and in Captain Blackford. We saw how he handled that ship.

Farrell: Those tugs should never have gone to sea. We had to show some of the people in the engine rooms of those tugs how to start their engines. First, they lost all their fresh water, and then they lost most of their food. We'd have to come alongside and supply them with water and food. Some of those guys were so sick that they just stayed in their bed. They rode those things down just to get it over with. They were not navy ships; they were army ships. It was so bad that we just stopped—and you *never* stop a convoy—but we just stopped, to try to regroup. We knew there were people in the water, so we turned on the flashlights even though we were right off the French coast, which was occupied by the Germans. And we turned the lights on, which you *never* do.

War Diary (17 October 1944): Escorting advanced section of NY-119, with order from C.T.G. to take all vessels to Falmouth and originate all necessary traffic to shore authorities regarding this section. Out of T.B.S. range of C.T.G. 27.5 by 1600 and using 2410 kilocycles voice whenever necessary. Wind 18–35 knots. Sky overcast clearing for an hour giving the only information in two days on which to make landfall. Changed course. . . . Section now making good 5 knots with a following sea. All hands making better weather of it with the increase in speed. Estimated landfall on Bishop Rock at 0300 October 18.

Buchanan: It was so overcast we couldn't take a navigation reading. We had dead reckoning. That's what we were traveling on, dead reckoning. I was up on the bridge with the executive officer, Lieutenant Ross, and I saw a star. It was just a little gap in the sky, but I called his attention to it. We had just enough time for both of us to shoot it before the clouds covered it again. We both went down to the charts, and we both marked it up. It turned out our lines were next to each other. The captain came up on the bridge, and he radioed over to the commodore of the convoy what our position was. In another few days, when we came out of the storm, the commodore congratulated us because we were right on. I remember it so well. We got the sextant, and I took the time for Lieutenant Ross, and he took the time for me as we read it. And then we went to the charts, and we made the lines, and we were parallel to each other on the lines, so we figured we had it right. I felt kind of nice about that, that I could handle a sextant, because I knew the officers could do it, and I could do it too.

Lind (report): When the full violence of the storm on 18 October 1944 had sunk ST-511 and ST-720, and broken up all but one of the remaining tows, the numerous small, unattached craft were in imminent danger of also overturning and being lost. CTG 27.5 was now faced with the grave decision of attempting to keep the convoy intact and fighting out the storm together or detaching the small craft without adequate escort or service tug protection and sending them to the shelter of nearby land at their best speed. After carefully weighing all the facts and with predictions of still continued increasing high seas and wind it was decided to send the 20 unattached small craft, now in charge of the USS *MASON*. . . . Great credit for their safe arrival is due to the outstanding seamanship of Lieut. Comdr. W. M. Blackford, Commanding Officer, USS *MASON* . . . in keeping his flock of 20 small craft together and shepherding them in to safety.

DuFau: We had the most vicious experience with that ocean. You'd be surprised how damaging that water can be when it gets to acting up. We had more damage done to the convoy from that storm than from any contact with submarines. The actual experience of having a storm hit a convoy made us see just how *small* man was on that ocean, how small the ships were on that ocean. Our ship, our destroyer escort, would be caught in the trough at the bottom of a wave, taken up to the top, and we stood at the top of that wave for a second, then came down like a kid on a sliding board. That was the most frightening experience, to realize that we were out in an ocean acting up that way, and we had so little control over that ship. We were almost at its mercy, trying to steer that ship into the sea to keep a headway so that we could keep some type of control.

War Diary (18 October 1944): Escorting advance section of NY-119. MASON the only escort present. All other occupied attempting to bring in the tugs and barges of the convoy. Commanding Officer HMS PRETEXT acting as section Commodore. At 0010, ran out ahead to make landfall. At 0032, Bishop Rock sighted bearing 052 degrees, distance 22 miles. Landfall reported to Task Group Commander by voice radio. . . . Barometer falling rapidly with wind and sea increasing. . . . At about 1230, first ship entered Falmouth swift channel. During the morning the wind increased to 35 or 40 knots. Section began scattering badly with the danger that some vessels might be swept on past the harbor entrance; consequently [*Mason* sent urgent message] requesting immediate assistance from local escorts. Intercepted message from POWERS to Plymouth reporting the loss of barges and ST-720. Wind and weather became rapidly worse. HMS PRETEXT had no charts of Falmouth, so it was necessary to lead the section from buoy to buoy and between buoys to run back to the end of the column about seven miles astern to guide in any possible stragglers. Wind now blowing 50–60 in the gusts—visibility zero. It was necessary to run at seventeen knots to accomplish this;

consequently several welded seams in the deck carried away and two longitudinal strength members in compartment B-4 came adrift. This ship handled well at all times and showed little tendency to broach running before the seas which were by then quite high. Wind reached a maximum of 70–80 knots in the gusts at about 1400. All vessels of the advanced were successfully turned over to the local escort inside the bay at Falmouth by 1645. It was impossible to report this to C.T.G. 27.5 at the time as the regular antennae had blown away and it was necessary to rig a new one.

Divers: They claimed that those ships weren't built to take a seventy-degree roll. It was like the pendulum on a clock, with a graduated scale. There were so many degrees from dead center all the way up to ninety, which was flat over. And we made a seventy-degree roll! When we were on picket duty, we always had to change course. We never ran a straight course; we were always on a zigzag. Out of that pattern we would eventually come broadside to the waves. In the big, serious storm of convoy 119 there was this super wave. That wave hit us. I was in the chart room, in the wheelhouse, and the whole ship went over. I said, "Uh-oh, we're not going to make it this time!" She held there, held there. Finally, she lurched and came back up. I looked at the inclinometer; it said seventy degrees. A lot of guys, DE sailors, have told me, "You will never make a seventy-degree roll and come out from under it." I've seen guys brag at making forty- or forty-five-degree rolls. But we made a *seventy-degree roll,* and I saw it with my own eyes. It made a double impression upon me. That's why I can recall it to this day.

DuFau: There was a crack in a seam on the deck of the ship. A couple of men—damage control men—had to go up under storm conditions and weld that seam in the deck. The guys received some type of award for doing it under those conditions. Afterwards, the damage control officer said if we had ignored that seam, the ship could have split right across, because the rocking and pounding of the waves could have caused that ship to split. In fact, the navy did record cases where DEs split in half. Two destroyer escorts were hit by either mines or torpedoes, and they split. They took two half destroyer escorts, towed them to the navy yard in New York, and welded them together to make one. The destroyer escort was a fragile ship. It was an emergency-built ship to help combat submarines.

Lind (report): The USS MASON had been placed in charge of a separate unit of the convoy consisting of all the 14 Y-oilers, 4 ST Tugs, HMS ASTRAVEL and HMS PRETEXT on 17 October and directed to steam at their slowest safe speed as the speed of the main Convoy was now too slow for their safety. . . . At 180934Z the MASON sent an ETA at FALMOUTH at 1800. At 181303Z MASON sent a message to FALMOUTH: "REQUIRE IMMEDIATE ADDITIONAL ESCORT ASSISTANCE FOR ADVANCE SECTION NY119 OFF LIZARD HEAD X SECTION SCATTERED BADLY DUE TO HIGH SEAS". At 181514 CIC PLYMOUTH ordered HMS ROCHESTER and HMS SALADIN to proceed at best speed to the assistance of the MASON. At 181800 all 20 small craft of this unit were safe in FALMOUTH. No doubt many of these small craft and the lives of the men thereon were saved due to the untiring efforts and good seamanship displayed by Lt. Comdr. Blackford during the two days when the MASON alone shepherded them to safety.

Though the *Mason* had shepherded her small flock to safety, her own work was not over. No sooner had she delivered the ships to the harbor than she moved out again to rejoin the convoy and offer assistance. The *Mason* had been in Falmouth harbor less than two hours when the crew turned around and went back.

War Diary (18 October 1944): At 1645, HMS ROCHESTER and SALADIN (sloops) reported for duty and all three vessels put to sea in attempt to round up possible stragglers from main body of convoy which apparently passed Bishop Rock at about 1200 Z. Neither of the sloops was able to make headway against the seas and returned shortly thereafter. This vessel able to make good, four knots while making revolutions for twelve. No noticeable strain to our hull or engines during the part of the operation. LT-653 located at 2016 and given necessary instructions for entering port. Wind velocity decreased to 40–50 knots at midnight.

DuFau: Oh, we knew the English ships wouldn't come out because Buchanan and I were the signalmen during the exchange between our ships and their ships. First, we spent a half an hour or more exchanging information about who was the superior officer among the escort vessels, as to who would be in charge, commanding the vessels. Now, we had brought the convoy over the whole ocean, and they spent at least half an hour exchanging messages to decide who was in command of the overall convoy, who they had to take orders from! I remember there was one message about their officer, telling what his commission was and what year he received it.

The British ship was telling us what rank their officer held and what year he graduated! There was this exchange going on, and we were saying to ourselves, "Well, what the hell does that have to do with this convoy thing?" Then, by the time we got that squared away, and they accepted that our U.S. ship was in charge, they decided they were returning to harbor because the seas were too rough. We spread the word among the crew, "Do you believe a British navy ship said that the seas are too rough?" And we had brought the convoy over all this distance, and they couldn't come out and help us do the clean-up job!

It was a hell of an experience. It was shocking to us. But that made us feel *real* great as sailors—we had accomplished this! After all this history about how great the British navy was, they'd do a thing like that. It's not damning the whole navy, but these particular two ships made them look real bad. And we were very fussy about making *our* ship look good. We did everything we could.

Farrell: The water was coming through the deck onto the switchboards. We had to put canvas over the boards to divert the water away from the electricity. The British sent out fuel barges and refueled us. We went out, but the Brits wouldn't go. The British ships started out, and then they turned around and went back.

DuFau: The calm that was among the crew members in the midst of this conflict was remarkable. We would resort to trying to humor each other, rather than being in fear. But fear was there. Personally, I had reached a stage where I'd say, "Well, there's nothing we can do." There was no way to swim to get out of there because the ships couldn't come near each other, and the nearest line was straight down. So if the end came, we'd just hope that we were at peace with our Maker, that we could survive. We'd joke with each other, back and forth, to cover up the fact that we were all *scared to death*, every one of us.

Lind (report): The USS MASON in company with HMS ROCHESTER and SALADIN started to return to the assistance of the tugs and barges immediately after delivering the 20 small craft to safety at FALMOUTH. Shortly after they emerged from the channel and began plowing into the 40-foot seas both British Sloops refused to proceed further and returned to anchorage. The plucky USS MASON, although already damaged to the extent of having several welded seams open in her decks and two longitudinal strength members in compartment B-4 adrift together with her radio antennae blown down during her fight against the sea in bringing in the 20 small craft during the day, effected emergency repairs and persisted in continuing to rejoin. CTG directed the C.O. MASON to slow to safe speed, take any safe course, turn back if he considered it advisable, but Captain BLACKFORD insisted on going back to rejoin the convoy. CTG 27.5 considers the performance of the USS MASON, her Commanding Officer, Officers and men outstanding and recommends that this ship be given a letter of commendation to be filed in the record of each officer and man on board that vessel.

From the eighteenth through the twenty-first the *Mason* stayed at sea, fighting the terrible storm to rescue the tugs, recapture the barges, and assist the other DEs. She was ordered to take shelter in Plymouth harbor as another storm swept through, but she was under way again on the twenty-fourth of October, headed for the French coast to recover salvageable barges. Finally, on the twenty-seventh, the *Mason* arrived in Plymouth harbor.

Graham: Our Captain Blackford requested that the crew of the ship be given a commendation, a letter of commendation, but the navy didn't want to hear it. They refused it. We put the letter that Captain Blackford had sent to the Navy Department, making the request, on the bulletin board. Someone removed it for a souvenir, I think. We put it on the bulletin board right outside the radio shack, and someone stole it. But Blackford had requested a letter of commendation. The navy gave medals to the commodore of the convoy instead of giving it to certain ships.

The crew never knew that, in addition to their captain's request, the commander of the convoy had also recommended that they be honored. The official navy report that reveals this information came to light only during the writing of this book. No letters of commendation were ever issued.

DuFau: The most hurtful experiences for me were not in the United States but in Plymouth, England. At that time it was one of the most bombed cities in England. You could see the front of the building, but behind it was an empty shell, blasted out. We went ashore because we had heard about a Red Cross canteen. The word was out among the sailors that they served Coca-Cola and hot dogs and mustard. We hadn't had Coca-Cola and hot dogs and mustard since we'd left the States. And I think that about three or four of us were together, found the canteen, and went up the steps, excited about getting hot dogs. This lady told us *it wasn't our canteen,* that our canteen was a few blocks down. It was such a slap in the face. All we wanted was hot dogs and Coke, and we ran into this.

So she directed us to a canteen that was operated by a black woman who was a USO lady. It was on the ground floor of a building that had been bombed. They had this canteen, and what it consisted of was a pool table and, for refreshments, cookies and Kool-Aid, lemon-flavored Kool-Aid. That was what we had for refreshments. And the USO lady apologized to us for offering something like this. She said when she volunteered to be in that duty, she didn't think she would be in such a position. But her hands were tied; that's all she had to work with.

Grant: From Plymouth I took a train to London, and I was a little shocked. In London they had a separate USO for blacks. It seemed a bit of a step back. Segregation was understandable in parts of the States, but over there! I asked them, "How could you? How could you? I don't understand. How could you do this?"

But they said, "The United States is paying us so we have to do what they say." They were paying them for that facility, so the people said, "OK, if they say we have to segregate you, we have to do it."

I said, "Why do you have to do it? This is your country. You could tell them to go jump in the lake or something." They didn't like that.

Watkins: We had some run-ins in England with some of the other sailors. They didn't seem to appreciate us, in some way, and I guess we didn't appreciate them.

They had told the people, "Be careful of those guys; they've got tails." We had one fight in England; it didn't last long. But some of the white guys resented us. Our sister ship was the *Bermingham,* and it was all white. They gave us more trouble than anybody else. Some of the officers praised us, and the white enlisted guys didn't like it at all. But we didn't let that bother us.

The only ones I remember fighting with were the marines—the white marines! I think it was Plymouth, England. We didn't have much of a fight. They busted the glasses in the pub, but it didn't last long.

Contacts

Convoy duty demanded that each man concentrate on his job, which left little time for personal conflict. But when the *Mason* reached port after escorting convoy NY-119, submerged tensions surfaced. All of the chief petty officers were white. The chiefs were supposed to instruct the men in their divisions so they could advance in rate and eventually replace the chiefs. Indeed, by the time the *Mason* was decommissioned, the chief petty officers were black, and men like Lorenzo DuFau and Gordon Buchanan had first-class ratings. But some of the chiefs had a different idea of their place on the ship.

Graham: We were changing tradition. I got the feeling that some of the chiefs just didn't want to be seen as opening the door to let us in. It was like, "If I can stop them advancing on my watch, no one could blame me." They just wanted to put up barriers. Anyone who's lived under prejudice learns to read people. You don't need words; there's a thousand ways of knowing. These chiefs were there to help us, but some took advantage. The chief radioman was the worst. The hatred was too deep in him to let him do his navy job. He was the worst kind of southern cracker you can come by, put it that way. He never taught us anything.

DuFau: The captain met with all the chiefs separately. He wanted to discuss any friction on the ship. Now this meeting was confidential, but we found out what was said. There's no such thing as a secret in the navy. Any two people knowing something, and there's no more secret. The yeomen were like the secretaries and would type up the report on the meeting. We heard what went on. The chief radioman told the captain that everything would be all right if we were kept in our place. So the captain said, "What do you mean 'in their place'?" He answered that they didn't want any of us up around the chief petty officers' quarters. Now you had to walk through their quarters to get to the forward anchor section. We'd have to go there to chip and paint or to work on the anchor. The chiefs wanted us to go over the deck and climb down through a hatch instead of walking through the quarters. Imagine trying to do that in a rough sea. But they wanted to be isolated, to make their quarters like the captain's wardroom. Now, this was against navy regs, but they wanted to take advantage of their position. And they were laying out demands to the captain—what he *had* to do to keep them happy.

Garrison: I came from the South, from an intensely segregated situation. And yet I had no difficulty whatsoever working with white people. Remember, we ate in the same quarters as the white petty officers—except for the chiefs. All of us on the *Mason* crew were intensely interested in doing our best and being our best. That was our focus. I wish you could see some of the messages we copied during some of the most vicious storms. You can imagine, sitting at a typewriter, and the typewriter's coming up in your face. And you're typing it *neatly*, without making an *error*. Initialing it at the end. It's amazing how proficient people can be under these adverse circumstances. But we couldn't get the credit for what we did unless the chief approved. I remember an investigation of the radio shack was ordered because radiomen were not being advanced as fast as the other ratings were.

Graham: The chief radioman would come into the radio shack, change the frequency, and just walk out—never telling us what he was doing or why. He treated us like we weren't there. So when we heard about what they were telling the captain, we weren't surprised.

DuFau: The very next day after the meeting, scuttlebutt had it, "Go hang out on the boat deck. The yeoman is about to read some orders that you want to hear." The yeoman called the chiefs up to the quarterdeck and read their orders. We were in Brooklyn Navy Yard at that time. The yeoman read the chiefs' orders; they were being transferred from our ship to the receiving station in New York for future orders. At that time all available chiefs were being shipped to the West Coast, because they wanted them for the landing craft for the invasion of Japan. So it was kind of shaky for a guy to be floating around at that time. But the captain transferred them off the ship the very next day after that meeting. As the chief radioman was leaving that ship, he turned and just spewed out his hatred to the men. He said he didn't give a damn what happened to us. He hoped when we got out there in that ocean, some submarine would hit us and destroy every one of us. One of the guys yelled back, "We *love* you, chief." And we all took it up. We hollered, "We love you. We love you." That was about the final word for him. He stomped off that ship and just went away.

The deck log notes the departure of the men, and Captain Blackford's letter to his parents seems to allude to a change for the better— perhaps that the navy's Bureau of Personnel had agreed to step up the promotion of black chiefs.

Blackford (letter to his parents): USS MASON (DE 529) 18 December 1944: Have just completed a series of conferences with the Bureau of Personnel who are giving us every possible assistance with our problems. Everything is remaining in good shape, but there is difficulty in getting qualified men for certain highly technical billets. In some cases it is all but impossible to train technicians aboard, so the schools are being combed. Morale has been on a gradual upswing for several months now, and I understand we have an excellent reputation for operations. The job is becoming increasingly more pleasurable, as we have acquired quite a group of officers now, including our own disbursing officer and doctor. The officers are really good, . . . by coincidence they are all far above average in intelligence, if not in experience. The Navy has changed a regulation or two and we now carry about 100 cases of beer aboard (for the men to use ashore overseas). We have a big Christmas celebration planned if it isn't too rough, and I am supposed to preach a sermon! The eventual policy for Negro personnel has been finally decided upon, but I could not discuss it here. In any case we are to get more cooperation than in the past, which is good.

The *Mason* had just completed exercises in which the crew's performance had been classified "Very Good." On both December 10, 1944, and December 13, 1944, the war diary describes target practice and antisubmarine runs in which observers classified results as "Very Good." An observer for the navy's personnel bureau, Charles Dillon, had inspected the crew. As in many instances, however, the navy's interest differed from the story the *Mason*'s crew were living. The bureau would judge the crew of the *Mason* in terms of chain of command: Could black petty officers enforce discipline? Would black enlisted men obey white officers? Judgments seem to have been made arbitrarily; there is little discussion of the actual duties the *Mason* performed, and yet Morris MacGregor, Jr., reports that the navy concluded that "black petty officers could not enforce discipline" and "black sailors did not respond well when assigned to all black organizations under white officers."*

Of course, there was tension when white petty officers made insulting demands or treated their men with contempt. The deck log of the *Mason* records the usual number of captain's masts and usual punishments for the kind of offenses common to every ship— lateness, oversleeping, absence from duty station, insubordination. James Graham remembers that sometimes a rated man would have to give an order to a nonrated man, who was also a friend. But obedience was expected. "We were all brothers," Graham recalls, "but if you had to, you put someone on report for not doing his job. You had to, or the ship would be jeopardized." The deck log has neither too many nor too few offenses. Bill Farrell, the officer in charge of the proceedings, says that the *Mason* had good discipline; the captain was neither too lenient nor overly strict.

DuFau: We policed each other. We'd tell a guy, "Now don't make Big Bill mad." He could come down on you. But mostly we just didn't want to disappoint him. Plus, it was to our interest that everyone did his job so things would go smoothly. Like the time the guy who was water tender wanted to go "over the hill." We were in port and he met a girl—that happened. He moved in with her and decided that was it; he was just going to stay put. He didn't think anybody would look for him. But if the ship left without him, he'd be in serious trouble; that was desertion. We went up to Harlem to find him. But it wasn't just because we didn't want him to get in trouble. No. It was because he was the

* From *Integration of the Armed Forces 1940–1965* by Morris J. MacGregor, Jr. (Center of Military History, U.S. Army, 1985), p. 78.

best at working the evaporators! He just knew how to keep those things going so we had fresh water twenty-four hours a day. We wanted that water! So we went up to Harlem and found him and brought him back. I knew him growing up in New Orleans. He'd fix our bikes and roller skates. He was just good mechanically. We needed him for those evaporators.

Captain Blackford appreciated the diverse talents his men brought to their jobs, and they respected him. His sister Sally Bruce married a naval officer, Marvin McClatchy, who served with Bill Blackford in the Aleutians. As do most officers who saw Blackford handle a ship at sea, McClatchy mentions his seamanship first. "He could just make a ship do what it was supposed to do." This was particularly important in the duty they shared—clearing mines. But Sally remembers most clearly Blackford's enthusiasm for the *Mason*.

Sally Bruce Blackford McClatchy: My husband was stationed in New York in the third Naval District before he went to the Pacific. When Bill's ship was in port he would come to dinner. He was very proud of his ship, very enthusiastic.

Marvin McClatchy: In the navy I went into, Negroes were only allowed in the servants rating—mess men, stewards. So the *Mason* was a brand-new thing, and Bill was very upbeat about it. He said the men were doing a good job. He was very favorably disposed.

Sally Bruce McClatchy: Bill was interested in how individual the men were, even how different each looked from the other. He said he'd like to learn more about African history, about the various tribes, and see what the connections might be.

Blackford was determined that his ship be treated as any other and respected for the job the crew did. As a reserve officer he was not part of navy politics, and he expected the *Mason*'s record to speak for itself. The crew, too, were interested in getting on with their duties and resented any attempts to be "Put under a microscope."

Graham: An officer from the Navy Department came on board to survey the guys, to see how they were doing, to monitor our activities. He was one of the navy inspectors, or observers. But when we'd see these guys coming from one direction, we went the other direction because we didn't want to be bothered. And most of the other officers who came aboard, came aboard more or less to learn. But I didn't like that. I was just the average guy. I was in the navy, and we were supposed to do this job. And I did it. As far as the politics was concerned, I didn't give a hoot.

Young: ABOARD THE USS MASON AT SEA—(Delayed)—This destroyer escort is doing two very good jobs for her country at the same time. One of them is helping a number of other similar fighting ships to get vital war goods to our armies in Europe.

The other is a job which the rest of the DEs in this task force do not have the opportunity to perform. Only the *USS MASON* with its mixed crew—largely colored—has the chance to demonstrate how easily workable, even on a warship hunting down Nazi U-boats, are the principles of democracy when given a fair trial.

That is not the mission of the *Mason* on its first combat voyage. The Navy sent it out here to do a fighting job; nothing more. But because it drew on white chief petty officers and a few white rated men with prior experience on warships to complement the crew, the Navy also created, no doubt entirely without design, a proving ground or floating laboratory.

Here is being tested the ability of its men in uniform to live and work peacefully and harmoniously and effectively, irrespective of previously applied patterns of separation. Here is being produced the evidence that Americans of all backgrounds and all complexions can and will settle down to the business of fighting together against a common enemy when they understand that it is the intent of the high command that they do so.

In most respects this is just another U.S. warship. The crew goes about its appointed tasks according to the book. Bunks in the crew's quarters are assigned according to sections in which the men work rather than their racial identity. The idea that there is any difference between the white and colored members doesn't have much chance of advancement below decks where the handful of white sailors sleep across from, above or below Negro bluejackets.

The chow hall is another demonstration of this. There are no white or colored tables. The men line up for their meals, first come first served, and sit where there is a vacant seat to eat them. . . .

Any other arrangement obviously would carry over into the way these men work and fight together. Such an effective and high-spirited team could not exist otherwise.

What racial separation there [is] on the *Mason* is unintentional and unavoidable. Standard practice on all Naval vessels provides the chiefs with their own sleeping quarters and their own mess. On the *Mason* all the chiefs are white.

Traditional Navy policy also draws a distinct line of demarcation between enlisted men and commissioned officers. Naturally, the staterooms and wardrooms where the officers eat are separated from facilities for the crew. Again, on the *Mason*, all the officers are white.

A good bit of the success of the *Mason* in carrying out this unassigned mission can be traced to the straight thinking of the commanding officer, Lt. Comdr. William M. Blackford, of Seattle, Wash. He regards his ship just like any other of the hundreds of destroyer escorts roaming the high seas, and not as a problem child or an 'experiment.'

At one of the ports visited a base commander told a group of officers from all the escort vessels in our task force that he expected trouble when the *Mason* crew got 'on the beach' (that's Navy lingo for going ashore).

Captain Blackford (regardless of their rank all ship commanders are called 'captain') was quick and emphatic in refuting that statement. 'Trouble?' he said. 'Why, my men get into less trouble than do those from any other of these ships. You won't have to worry about my crew. They know how to behave.'

One evening while we were tied up at a base on the other side of the Atlantic, I went with Capt. Blackford to visit on another DE. In the conversation one of the officers said to him, 'And you do have a problem on your ship.'

I thought for a moment that the Skipper was really angry. He challenged the remark vigorously.

'What do you mean, problem on my ship? In fact, I have less of a problem than you do here. We get along swell, and we do our job without any trouble.'

'Of course,' said the other officer, going directly to another topic of conversation.

On several occasions Capt. Blackford had said to me with zeal and sincerity, 'I'm no crusader. I'm not out here to solve the race problem. I'm simply trying to run a good Navy ship.'

DuFau: We took care of each other. The morale among the crew was so great, it helped us. We didn't realize how much we depended on each other. A guy could be in low spirits sometimes; it's only natural. He's human. He'd get lonely or something like that. But we could read the expression on the guy's face. One guy would tell the others, "Leave so-and-so alone; don't bother him, don't bother him." Give him that quiet time to go through it. If you'd bother him, he would react pretty violently, because he was down in his spirit. But we would find some way to let him settle in it for awhile, but then one after another we'd start getting after him, kidding and joking, to break him out of it. Then he'd admit that he was feeling low. So we were able to get strength from each other.

Simple things boosted morale. The arrival of Cassin Craig as disburser made a difference. A Philadelphia native, Craig joined the ship in November.

Cassin Craig: I came on board in November of '44. I was one of a good many guys who were graduated from Harvard Business School as supply officers, and I just happened to be sent to the USS *Mason*. They did not have a supply and disbursing officer before I reported. They were very happy to have me because I had money that I could distribute to them every two weeks, and I could get certain equipment that was assigned to the Supply Department. We had a Pepsi Cola machine installed, but it didn't work very well because of the rolling of the ship. We could use it only when we were in port.

A Pepsi machine and a Christmas service and party, recorded in the log, marked the end of 1944.

Graham: We put together a service. Captain Blackford spoke. We sang carols. I have some of the carols we sang that first Christmas. And we had a special meal. We were on our way across.

War Diary (1 January 1945): En route Norfolk, Virginia, to Oran, Algeria, escorting convoy "UGS-64" with other escorts of Task

Force 64 (Captain BERDINE, USCG in BALCH (DD-363)–C.T.F.). Task Force Sixty-four consists of: (a) DesDiv 26–LIVERMORE (DD-429); EBERLE (DD-430); GULFPORT (PF-20), temporarily assigned); and (b) CortDiv 80–O'TOOLE (DE-527–Flag); POWERS (DE-528); MASON (DE-529); BERMINGHAM (DE-530); ANDRES (DE-45); and CHASE (DE-16). Escorts operating under C.T.F.-64's *SECRET OPERATION ORDER 8-44 of 19 December 1944.*

Roberts: I didn't get a real job in the navy until finally, one day, someone came to me and said, "Pack your gear in seagoing fashion." I got on the USS *Mason* and didn't get off until we got to Oran.

The navy's tradition of marking the New Year in verse was observed by W. W. Pitts.

Deck Log (1 January 1945):

00–04 Here in the beginning while it's so near,
    I wish you all a Happy New Year!

    Underway from Norfolk, the state of Virginny,
    In the U.S.A., the land of plenty.

    We're bound for a place called Oran, Algiers,
    Of the Frenchmen there, we have no fears.

    The "Boss" of this "gang," Task Force Sixty-Four,
    Is riding the BALCH, and he knows the score.

    This "Gang" is made up, if you're interested, matey,
    Of DesDiv two-six and CortDiv Eighty.

    Of course the Coast Guard must be along,
    They sent the GULFPORT to sing their song.

    This "Gang" is escorting merships by the score
    It's known as convoy UGS Sixty-Four.

    Zero plus nine five is base course, that's true,
    As onward we sail o'er the ocean so blue.

    The speed we are making keeps us lookin' alive,
    Given in knots, it is nine point five.

With fifteen knots as standard speed set,
We're making two-thirds, but we're not there yet.

In order to stay on station right,
Three on five turns we're doing tonight.

Two main engines are runnin'—hear 'em Sport?
Number two on the starboard, number four on the
port.

In position three is where we stand,
Thus able to screen on the starboard hand.

"In Disposition Baker" our Commander cried,
"On plan Two Able I did decide."

"In case you're interested in who made same,"
"You're talking to the one who's to blame."

As the old year has departed, and the New Year has
begun,
On the war cruising watch stood section one.

The quartermaster on watch is a poet of rare wit,
And here I copy just as he "writ":

2356–: "Four one five" came to the wheel
For back into position we must steal.

0008–: Now the turns are three twenty, and there they will
stay,
Unless Lieutenant KITTS has more to say.

0014–: The Captain called, 'cause he couldn't be near
To wish the O.O.D.'s a "Happy New Year."

0345–: When this watch was over, together we cried,
"Tho we didn't par Whitman, My! How we tried."

Deck Log (1 January 1945):

16–18   Round and round the clock hands go,
The hours pass, but very slow.
I won't say much, tho I could say more,
For this short watch, just—steaming as before.
One other thing I'd better add,

In case it interests some other lad,
At seventeen ten by the wheel house clock,
To three twenty five the turns we did rock.

DuFau: We were crossing in a convoy, going from 1944 into 1945. We were asleep somewhere at sea. It hit midnight and on the loudspeaker we heard, "Happy New Year!" One guy started cursing *right and left*! He was so broken-hearted. Being away from home was on our minds, and the guy on the loudspeaker just sharpened the *edge* of it.

War Diary (2 January 1945): Screening as before. 0830–Sonar contact bearing 190 degrees proved to be a school of fish. . . . Consistent reports of enemy submarine in the approaches to the Straits of Gibraltar have been received for the past week. All necessary precautions have been taken as we are entering this area.

War Diary (3 January 1945): Screening as before. 0313–All hands at General Quarters investigating sound contact. Contact grew mushy and bearing widened to 35 degrees at 1000 yards, this combined with poor traces and erratic plot led to negative evaluation. . . . 1251–Casablanca section broke off and departed with French (PC) escorts. 2308–All hands at General Quarters assist BALCH in sonar contact. Contact proved false. At about 2100, received an urgent message from Flag Officer Gibraltar that a Mership in GUS-63 then about 60 miles ahead of us had been torpedoed at 1805 on this date. Additional air coverage for this convoy arrived shortly thereafter.

Graham: We knew there were U-boats around. Not only had a ship been sunk, but at night we could pick up U-boats transmitting to each other. Peters could identify German transmitting right away. They would transmit differently than we did. They were slower than we were, so it wasn't what we were accustomed to hearing.

We would know that there were Germans in the immediate area. When we were going through the Straits of Gibraltar, the convoy in front of us had had ships torpedoed, and the convoy behind us was torpedoed. But we were never torpedoed. We dropped a lot of depth charges, we killed a lot of fish—real fish—but we never did get a German sub.

Watkins: When we'd go to Africa, we'd have to go through the Straits of Gibraltar. So then the convoy would have to narrow out. It would have to single out to go through. Then DEs had to stay out and screen.

Once, the U-boats got a ship in the convoy ahead of us. Then they got a ship in the one behind. We were fortunate. We didn't lose any coming through the straits.

Craig: Off the (Atlantic) coast of Spain there's a shelf that goes into the Atlantic that's about 150 feet deep. The submarines could lie on the bottom there without being detected. The pressure increases as you go down, and they could go down only 200 feet, but if they could lie on that shelf, they could shut off their engines and be completely undetectable.

Graham: That [Gibraltar] was definitely a hot spot. The Germans would sit around and wait for us. Ships were sunk ahead of us and behind us. We would get that information in the radio shack. It was very narrow. They could sit there and wait for you.

Garrison: At sunset the captain would call everybody to general quarters because that was the time when the submarines were more likely to attack. We also had a gun that was called the "Ready Gun." It had shells in it, and all you had to do was trigger it, and that would give you time to get the other guns ready. There was a crew on that gun twenty-four hours a day.

Deck Log (11 January 1945): 00–04 Underway from Oran, Algeria, to Hampton Roads, Va., screening convoy GUS-64 under orders of CTG 60.11 in USS BALCH (DD-363), in company with USS O'TOOLE, USS John J. POWERS, USS John M. BERMINGHAM, USS GULFPORT. . . . At 0010, sound contact bearing 295 degrees True, range 2400 yards—commence run. 0014–Contact classified as non-sub—did not fire depth charge pattern.

Buchanan: I was on the bridge at this time, and sonar said that they had a contact. Sonar is when you're tracking something underwater; radar is when you're tracking something above the water. I was on the flying bridge. There were to be no lights on, not with a sub around, so I wasn't up on the signal bridge. I heard the sounds; I had had sonar training in the navy. I was listening, and then, all of a sudden, radar says, "We've got our contact." Then radar says, "Lost contact."

Gordon: I had come on duty at quarter of twelve, almost midnight. Within about five minutes I picked up this contact at three thousand yards. I recognized from all my training that this was a classic submarine contact. It had all of the indications. We had what we called the Varying Deviation Indicator, which showed the movement of the objects, plus we had the Doppler effect and the sound of the echo. This one was a classic. It was quite easy to hear; anybody in the vicinity could hear the echo. We sounded general quarters.

War Diary (11 January 1945): At 0010 made sonar contact bearing 295 degrees, range 2400 yards. Commanding Officer, Executive Officer and ASW Officer reported to their battle stations immediately and made all preparations for a depth charge attack. CTG 60.11 notified immediately by T.B.S. Contact was then evaluated as non-sub due to mushy echoes, narrow target, lack of bearing movement or Doppler, erratic recorder traces and no appreciable movement on DRT plot.

At 0015 made radar contact bearing 140 degrees distance 1500 yards. Sound contact was made on the same bearing at 1200 yards. This "pip" bore such remarkable resemblance to periscopes seen during training exercises that the decision was made to attack regardless of the previous evaluation.

Buchanan: Sonar says, "We picked it up. We got it!" And we started tracking for it. They called the captain to come up. Everybody went to battle stations. That was the best time. I said, "Oh, man, we got a submarine out here."

We had been tailing the convoy. No lights, just some stars in the sky. Pitch black. And I'm listening to it. We're finding it and we're losing it. The radar would pick it up, find it, and lose it. And we would track right in on it. The captain kept going. The depth charges were all set.

According to the war diary, all hands then manned battle stations, full speed was rung up, and depth charges were set on fifty feet. The task group commander was notified of these details, and the USS *O'Toole* was delegated to assist.

Peters: My battle station was in the radio shack. Whenever we went in there, I would put on the speaker phones to listen to the communication that was going on around the ship. I heard the sonar man calling ranges and bearings. They had a speaker on their sonar equipment as well as having phones, so I could hear the echoes back and forth from the sonar as he was calling ranges and bearings.

Then, all of a sudden, everything just went crazy. Guns started going off. Depth charges started going off. We had one kid in our radio shack who had just come aboard for that trip. He had never heard a gun. We hadn't had any gunnery practice with him aboard. He went berserk. He wanted out of that radio shack. We had to restrain him.

Gordon: I had a firing button. It was my job to push the button when it was time to fire the depth charges. So just before we got to the target, I pushed the button. The first depth charges were dropped and the K-guns were fired.

Buchanan: We shot off the depth charges, the K-guns were going, and oh, it looked like a big, yellow Christmas tree, a huge Christmas tree. I'm standing up there, and I'm forty feet off the water on a ship, a fourteen-hundred-ton ship, and I feel like somebody hit me with a baseball bat under my feet. And I was stuck on top of it. We dropped all these depth charges, and they're going off all over the place. And we hit it. Now you *want* to hit a submarine. You want to crash into it. If you got one, you want to make sure it's a kill.

Farrell: We aimed for him, were going to ram him, because we had a reinforced bow. We sent out the hedgehogs. We went in to ram and hit this thing. A millisecond before we hit, they rolled a full pattern of depth charges, which is eleven depth charges.

When we hit the thing, whatever it was, it was big enough and buoyant enough so that the whole bow of the destroyer went up in the air. It cleaned off everything underneath the ship. It cleaned off the sonar, it cleaned off the pit log,* and it also hit one of our propellers. We were up in the air, and then we came down.

War Diary (11 January 1945): At 0021 a heavy shock was felt forward, speed was not materially reduced and charges were dropped on orders of chemical recorder. Lookouts reported wreckage floating down both sides of the ship. At 0023 changed speed to full for new attack, giving O'TOOLE a range and bearing to the contact. At 0028, further amplifying report made to CTG and orders received to rejoin in 60 minutes if contact was not regained.

Farrell: Hitting that thing slowed the ship down. You have to go fifteen knots before you drop depth charges to get away from

---

* Short for pitometer log, a device that indicates the speed of a ship and distance run by measuring water pressure on a pitot tube projected outside the ship's hull.

them. It slowed us down enough so that we weren't going fifteen knots. The depth charges went off. Now the whole *stern* of the ship was up in the air.

It was utter chaos for a little while. I got a call from the bridge. "Bill, why the hell did you stop?" They had the pit log. It showed that we were not going.

I looked at the engine revolution counters on the thing and said, "Well, maybe you stopped, but we're still going." I thought we'd been cut in half. Except, if we had been cut in half, how could I be talking to him on the telephone? But you don't think of all those things.

Peters: We had slammed into something, and everything got quiet. The lights went out, and it was just completely silent. Then, eventually, the skipper came on the PA system and said, "This is your captain speaking. I think we got red-dog." We referred to the German wolf packs as "red-dog." So we were all jubilant. We had sunk a German submarine!

Gordon: We hit it, we hit this object. I felt it roll under the ship. I knew it had to be a submarine, because I felt it roll as it went under the ship. It wrecked the sonar because the sonar part hung down under the ship. After it damaged that, I had no more control over it.

Buchanan: Now I have to go down to the signal bridge. DuFau is on the signal bridge. There's this officer leaning over and talking to us. They want it lit up, but they don't want it lit too long. So we turn on a twelve-inch light. It lit up the whole ocean, and I said, "Oh, Lord, if that's a submarine, we've had it." Because if they were sitting there underneath us, and they saw us . . . I grabbed a shield to turn it down to a six-inch light.

Divers: When we hit it, everything rattled. I was thinking, "I wonder how cold that water is." Then everything was quiet, and all I kept hearing was, "Barracks clear! Repair One, Repair One." They had to send a party to check for damage up forward.

Divers: I didn't have my life preserver when we hit.

Watkins: Didn't you wear the belts?

Divers: I had the belts, but I got tired of wearing them because you never knew when you might go down.

Watkins: We had this belt of rubber a few inches wide, and you put it around you.

Divers: You know, I carried that thing the whole time I was on the *Mason,* and when I got off the ship, I brought it with me. I said,

"Let me see this thing, how it works." I broke that thing, and nothing happened. It didn't inflate!

Buchanan: They said, "Okay, light it up again." So they're right above me and they're telling me what to do, and I light it up again, and I see these huge beams sticking out of the water. *Huge* beams. I've never seen beams like that even here when they're doing construction. And we realized we were over some sunken derelict, and we had to get off of it. We were stuck on it! And we backed off. We managed to shake ourselves loose and back off of it.

Gordon: I never questioned that we had hit a submarine. I never heard any different. As a matter of fact, the skipper notified the crew over the loudspeaker. He said, "It looks like we got red-dog." We showed the lights only long enough to see that there was wreckage, and then they turned the lights out. By that time in the war, the submarines were operating in multiple units— wolf packs. If you sank a submarine, while you were gloating over your kill another submarine would sink you. So we didn't keep the lights on long; just enough to see wreckage.

But we never got credit for a kill, and I often wondered why. And now I hear the story has come out in recent years that it was a wooden barge of some kind. But I never heard that as long as we were aboard the *Mason*. That's something new.

History has proven that in the other military services, any real accomplishments by a black unit were somewhat covered up and put on the back burner. So this was not publicized properly like it would have been done for other ships. They didn't want to give the black enlisted men the credit like they did the others. If they had given credit, perhaps we would have been looked at differently as a race after the war. I am totally bewildered that it's been almost fifty years since the ship was commissioned, and the average public doesn't know that we ever existed. I still ask myself why.

The men of the *Mason* still argue the question when they meet— Was it a sub? Did they get red-dog? Most of them think not, and the official version concurs. But those who are convinced they did remain resolute.

War Diary (11 January 1945): Illumination by searchlight revealed plainly that the target was wooden derelict, probably a barge about 100 feet by 50 feet. This was reported at 0046. Sound gear and pit log found to be inoperative as a result of the collision. This was reported at 0105 and orders received to take station astern for balance of the night.

Buchanan: We had cut into it pretty deep. We damaged our bow. Water was rushing in. But the guys got mattresses to plug up the hole and made a good watertight thing. Our sonar gear was down. It was bent up under the ship.

And on the way back, we put the pit log on. We knew the Germans were listening for us all the time, so we had to keep the pit log going. That was the only thing that kept the submarines away from us.

Divers: There was a sonar contact, and they said it was a submarine. I know one guy, a sonar guy, who swears up and down that it was a submarine. He even wrote to the German admiralty, to the German government, to find out whether at that date and time there had been a submarine missing. But the official line is that we collided with a barge, with one of the barges that we had tried to sink on convoy NY-119.

We collided with something. It took all our sonar gear off. We bent one of the screws. We didn't have any protection. I was on the bridge all the time, so I know. We didn't have any way to detect submarines the exact same way the sonar did.

War Diary (11 January 1945): The newly installed manual control for the pit log proved to be of the utmost value to C-I-C during the latter part of this operation. It was cut in immediately after it was discovered that the pit log swordarm had been damaged and by using the RPM speed scale in the pilot house, the quartermaster was able to inform the C-I-C room of all changes in speed. As a result of this a good C-I-C plot was possible for directing "observant" and lost contact procedure. The extent of damage to the sound gear was not realized until after the target was identified; this included damage to the retraction assembly beyond repair at sea. After-steering helmsman reported excessive while returning to station.

MASON's visual to CTG 60.11 at 1022 gave report of damage. CTG's visual 1044 ordered MASON to proceed to Bermuda at best possible speed for emergency repairs and to rejoin as soon as possible, reporting departure to proper authorities when 100 miles from convoy. At 1045 departed from convoy for Bermuda via great circle route course 280 degrees speed 13 knots, port shaft secured to eliminate vibration.

Farrell: We reported to the commodore of the convoy that we couldn't maintain speed. The ship was jumping around, and we couldn't maintain speed. We had to make some emergency repairs. First, they detached one of the DEs to escort us, to screen us while we made repairs. But we couldn't do it fast enough. They had the DE rejoin the convoy and told us to go to Bermuda.

Divers: We had to leave the convoy. We had to limp back by ourselves.

Watkins: I don't know. It was a little slower than we ordinarily traveled because it had only one screw.

Divers: It didn't seem scary to us at that time because we were young and crazy. We didn't know any better.

Watkins: Young and goofy.

Divers: I'll tell you, if I had to do it over again, I'd think twice, since I *know* I got sense now. But we were all kids.

Farrell: Now, here we're going along, except, number one, we have no way of telling if there are any submarines down there, because we had no sonar—that was knocked off. We didn't have a pit log, and we still had a bent propeller. We were finally able to make some temporary repairs, so we could come back on one shaft. We didn't sleep *too* good until we got to Bermuda.

Garrison: I was glad we went back, because Bermuda meant warm weather, probably short duty. I wasn't scared at all. I'm not boasting, but I had confidence enough in that crew. If a submarine surfaced, and they didn't have their guns operating the minute they surfaced, they wouldn't have had a chance with the *Mason.* The most foolish thing that he could have done would be to surface. Now, if he stayed under, submerged, he might have a chance. But with the sonar, we should pick up the torpedo, and might be able to move out of the way. We had about nine 20-millimeter guns. We had one gun called the 1.1, which had four barrels, firing simultaneously. It could fire horizontally or vertically. And you could rake a submarine. I mean, anybody coming topside wouldn't stand a chance! For that reason, I didn't fear at all. But I supposed if he hit us in the wrong place, hit the magazines, for example, *we* could blow up.

The navy trains you to be anxious. You are already prepared, but you are anxious to do what you're trained to do. So that sort of lessens the fear when you have to do what you're supposed to do. And when that alarm goes off, you are ready to face whatever comes, whether it be a submarine or an aircraft or another vessel. You're just trained that way.

Graham: It's after it's over and you're secure from general quarters that you start thinking, "What if that was a submarine that came topside and started shooting at me?" Then you'd start shaking in your boots.

War Diary (19 January 1945): Underway at 0840 for St. George's Harbor, fueled to capacity, and had local diver inspect sound dome and shafts. Inspection showed conditions satisfactory for trip to New York.

Buchanan: There was this big harbor at Hamilton, Bermuda. I had to go ashore to pick up my prisoner. One of our guys was in the brig there. He'd been sent there while we were repairing the ship. I can't remember what he'd done.

The *U-505* was there, a German submarine. The only thing I kept thinking was, "Why wasn't I lucky enough to capture that?" Oh, I would have been high on the hog then. When I got down to the barracks that the marines originally had, there were navy guys at the door. They were security for the crew of the *U-505*. But I went in not knowing *what* I was walking into; I was just there to pick up my prisoner. I saw these fellows sitting at a table all playing cards. These were the Germans that had been captured. The American sailors told me to go up the road and find where the marines were keeping U.S. prisoners.

So I walked away from there. The Germans were playing cards, but when I found my prisoner, he was cleaning the decks, scraping the decks. The navy security guards for the Germans just had 45s holstered, but the guys guarding our American sailor prisoners pointed rifles right at them. This turned me against the marines because of how they treated the navy guys. The fellow that I had to pick up told me later, "Boy, when I saw you at that door, I was *so* happy to see you. You don't know what went on in this place." So I got him back to the ship, and we went on with the convoy.

The divers in Bermuda went under the *Mason* to look at the ship, and they said we could get back to New York. We got back to New York and then got into the Brooklyn Navy Yard to straighten out the ship.

Steaming as Before

The *Mason* shepherded three more convoys across the Atlantic to Oran, Algeria, in February, March, and April 1945. The U-boats made their final frantic effort to impede the advancing Allies by relaying weather information to the German army as well as attempting to staunch the continuous procession of ships. The men found Algeria both exotic and welcoming. The war diary mentions the good facilities provided by the Mers el-Kébir port authorities. But even as the men picnicked on the beach, the poverty of the Algerian people disturbed them, and they devised ways to get around the rules against giving food to the people. As they made their way to Oran, however, more mundane matters—with their own chow—presented themselves.

Deck Log (8 February 1945): 16–18 Steaming as before. 1700–Inspected crew's chow consisting of unsavory and tough beef stew, very greasy fried potatoes, delicious beets, salad and cake. Biscuits also were served. Notified Captain, Executive Officer, Supply Officer, and acting commissary steward of unsatisfactory meal. Trouble tracked down to [the man], who cooked the offensive part of meal using his own methods of seasoning. [He] was reprimanded again this time for his careless preparation of crew's food. Supply Officer and commissary steward taking steps to prevent recurrences.

It is tempting to draw psychological implications from this incident. Imagine how men who still served in the servants ratings must have felt about those who had advanced to the seaman's branch. But the crew rejects such speculations. "He just acted mean sometimes. We set him straight."

The DEs had gone on the offensive: hunter-killer groups sank *U-248* in February and *U-866* in March. One of the DEs that attacked *U-866* was the USS *Menges* (DE-320). In May 1944, while rescuing sailors from the USS *Lansdale* (DD-426) after a German air attack, the *Menges* had been hit by the *U-371*. Though his ship was badly damaged and thirty-one of his crew were killed, Comdr. Frank McCabe refused to abandon his ship. The *Menges* was towed to Brooklyn Navy Yard where her aft section was joined to the stern section of the USS *Holder* to make one whole ship. The *Holder* had been torpedoed by German aircraft on April 11, 1944. The crew kept her afloat so she could be towed, first to Oran and then to New York. The salvageable parts of her forward hull were used for the *Menges*.

The stories of DE exploits encouraged the *Mason*'s crew to hope for their own U-boat kill. Contacts continued to alternate with the routines of shipboard life. Vigilance in the face of boredom was the particular challenge of escort duty.

Garrison: Let me explain about the submarine runs we were doing in the spring of 1945. Some were meant to divert the sub, and on some we were actually trying to sink them. The sonar men operated a machine that sent out an echo to a submerged object. You would measure the time between when the sound went out and hit the object and when it came back. That told us whether there really was a sub and how close the submarine was. Then we were called to general quarters. Every man manned his battle station. We would drop depth charges until we were sure that we had hit him, or he had gotten away. Sometimes we'd have what they'd call embarrassing runs. You didn't really mean to sink the sub as much as just run it away, get it out of there so that we could get on about our business.

When you really wanted to have a kill, the escort commander would assign two or three ships to stay for an hour or so more, if it was necessary, over the area where the depth charges had been dropped. We'd stay until we didn't get any more contact from him. Sometimes the U-boats sent out debris like oil or mattresses through the torpedo tubes. Anything to make us think we'd hit them, so we would go away. But if you really hit him, he had to come up. Once he surfaced, all the other guns were leveled on him.

Once we assisted a destroyer on a submarine attack, and we did see oil come up. But as I say, we didn't know whether this guy was faking it or whether it was a real hit. So after awhile, we were called off.

War Diary (28 February 1945): Screening as before. 0100–convoy commenced reducing front to three columns, MASON took station on port quarter. 0108–convoy course changed to 077 for passage through Straits of Gibraltar. 0539–Europa Point abeam. 0547–escorts relieved. MASON (senior) with POWERS and GULFPORT proceeded in formation and performed DesLant Gunnery practices, breeches buoy exercises, etc., throughout day while en route to Oran. 1527–Alboran Island sighted, . . . 2206, POWERS reported a human cry in the water. Area was thoroughly searched by all three ships without result. Muster of three ships showed all hands to be present. 2310, formation proceeded toward destination.

The men knew there were many human cries unheard and that the Mediterranean Sea had claimed the bodies of seamen since before history. But there were rescues too.

Divers: I recall one time in the Mediterranean when the convoy ahead of us lost a seaman, a Frenchman. We were at the rear of the convoy. They said, "Watch out for this guy." We spotted him. He had been in the water for twenty-four hours. We picked him up, but we didn't have to put him in sick bay or anything. He was just a remarkable specimen of a man.

War Diary (2–4 March 1945): Moored at Mers el-Kébir, Algeria, awaiting orders.

Deck Log (5 March 1945): 08–12 Moored as before. 0805–All final preparations made for Annual Military Inspection. Magazines open; smoking lamp out. 0825–Inspecting party headed by Comdr. Lind, ComCortDiv 80 and consisting of officers from the DE-528–POWERS aboard. AT 0845 all divisions called to quarters and Annual Military Inspection begun. Personnel inspection by Divisions, followed by cleaning station and material inspection ended at 0945 when all hands changed into the uniform of the day (dungarees) for Battle Problems.

Farrell: We passed all our inspections. In fact, I'd visit the other engineering officers and look in at their engine rooms. It's not for me to say ours was better, but I was pleased at the comparison. On the anniversary of our ship's commissioning, Captain Blackford awarded citations.

On the anniversary of the ship's commissioning the captain held a special mast to congratulate the men and to promote certain members of the crew.

In the period between convoys the *Mason* continued training exercises. Scuttlebutt said that the ship would be sent to the Pacific. The navy had decided to match the film made for the army by John Ford, *The Negro Soldier*, with *The Negro Sailor*. Camera crews came aboard the *Mason*. The beautifully shot footage of the ship and her men was supplemented by the story of a "typical Negro enlistee." When James Graham received a video copy of *The Negro Sailor*, he edited out the theatrical inserts, which are unrealistic and stereotypical. The film also shows that the majority of black men in the U.S. Navy were performing menial tasks.

War Diary (6 April 1945): 0635–underway with POWERS to exercise area. During morning made runs on bottomed submarine near Block Island and during afternoon conducted fighter director exercises. During day and on subsequent days until arrival Norfolk BuAer official Navy photographers made scenes for a forthcoming Navy motion picture titled "The Negro Sailor". Ship's officers and personnel gave them every possible assistance and cooperation. 1627–completed exercises and proceeded to moor State Pier, New London, at 1940.

CTG 60.11's visual dispatch 082150 ordered MASON (senior) to conduct remainder of exercises and report with group less MC COOK, 11 April 1945 at Hampton Roads. 0735–9 April, underway from anchorage to exercise area, 4 miles east Montauk Light. Submarine S-20 delayed near New London due to heavy fog. During morning while waiting for sub photographers were placed aboard POWERS and MASON made runs past POWERS for use in motion picture previously mentioned. At 100 S-20 arrived and ASW runs commenced at 1145 with POWERS and MC COOK. During afternoon creeping attacks were made. At 1500 submarine surfaced; proceeded to moor State Pier, New London at 1712.

Later in April the *Mason* began what would be her last overseas voyage.

War Diary (14 April 1945): 0445–underway to convoy anchorage Lynnhaven Roads. 0727–picked up mail from Convoy Commodore UGS 86, for delivery to New York section upon rendezvous. At 1146 abeam buoy XS; at 1249 passed mail to EL PASSO and EUGENE, who were escorting New York section of convoy. At 1440, commenced passing mail to each merchant ship of the New York section while the convoy was forming up. This entailed several difficult situations because the merchant vessels were continually changing course and speed during the mail passing, attempting to gain their proper convoy positions. At 2000, MASON ordered to patrol station #5 on starboard flank of convoy, which was formed up by this time, the two sections having merged.

War Diary (29 April 1945): Proceeding in column, course 097, speed 15, with POWERS, O'TOOLE, and EUGENE, from Europa Point to Oran. 0620–Isle d'Alboran light abeam, changed course to 088. At 1321, entered Oran swept channel and ordered ships in company to enter harbor independently to fuel. 1415–moored to fueling jetty and took on Diesel fuel to capacity. 1614–underway to moor at 1708 along jetty at Mers el-Kébir, Algeria.

Craig: When we went into Mers el-Kébir, Algeria, we had to go behind a concrete seawall that the French had built. The wind was blowing offshore with tremendous gusts, and none of the ships could dock. We were not the first one in line among the escorts; we were maybe the second or third. The first captain that went in just didn't know how to deal with this thing. As he tried to approach the seawall where we were to tie up, the ship kept sailing away. So Blackford says, "Let me go in first. I know how to handle this." What he did was, instead of having the ship go in sort of parallel to the dock, he headed straight for the dock. Then he got the crewmen to throw over the number one and number two lines. Then he brought the ship to a quick halt and swung it around on the front lines by backing down on the outboard engine. He showed the other ships how to do it. It was such a beautiful thing to see him handle that ship. You had to see it.

Farrell: Bill Blackford loved the navy. I think he was happier when we were at sea than when we were at port. Blackford was an excellent ship handler. He could take that DE and dock it just like you'd park a Chevrolet somewhere. He could almost put it in the space that you'd put a Chevrolet in. Many times we would come in, and if it wasn't too bad, he would take the ship right up to the dock. The crew would jump onto the dock and handle our own lines. He was excellent for handling the ship.

War Diary (30 April 1945): Moored inside breakwater Mers el-Kébir, North Africa, waiting instructions during layover period between UGS-86 and GUS-88 convoys. Crew on 50% shore liberty basis with some organized recreation parties. The Oran area provides excellent recreational facilities for enlisted men and the shore authorities cooperate with escort vessels to the greatest possible extent.

Farrell: I was the recreation officer. Sometimes at Oran we'd have a baseball game, and we'd take the beer out. We never drank beer on the ship. We'd have a picnic. We'd also tie the ships up together so we could have boxing on the fantail. I would go on the other DEs, the 527, 528, and see if anyone wanted to have a match. It was easy, because our ship had boxers at every weight. I had a lot of Golden Glove champions. We had something on the *Mason* that I doubt too many DEs had, a ship's band. The *Chicago Defender*, the newspaper in Chicago, gave us the instruments. We carried them on the ship.

Garrison: We went on liberty, and that's where we saw the women with the veils. We were told not to bother them at all. And of course, we didn't bother them, but we were curious. We wanted to know what was going on. They also had handmade leather goods there, and we bought boots, belts, pocketbooks.

In North Africa it seemed like everybody had money, currency. They had this scrip that was printed in Philadelphia! Even the kids had big bankrolls. So we would sell them cigarettes, Hershey Bars, sheets, any kind of linen. A lot of guys would go ashore with a hundred dollars U.S. and come back with what would be the equivalent of two thousand dollars U.S. in this scrip. Then they would change it into U.S. currency. But they put a stop to that, so that you could never bring back more than you went ashore with.

We had a good time in North Africa.

Buchanan: Mers el-Kébir was where the French used to have their warships. The British had sunk the French fleet there early in the war, when the French surrendered to the Germans. Their masts were still sticking up above water.

They had a little basketball hoop on the docks; well, it was a quay, really. And boy, we used to play basketball there all day long, as much as you could.

We weren't allowed in the Kasbah, but the army had a base nearby, and I said, "Let's try the back end. That has got to be open." So we jumped on an army truck, went up there, and just told the guy, "Stop, let us off." We jumped off. Mozell White, from Paterson, New Jersey, was . . . I wish I knew where he was, to ask him if he remembers this story.

But we got off, and we went into that little area there. We went and stopped in a couple of bars. We drank cognac. It don't take you long to get high on cognac. And then finally, as the sun started to drop a little bit, we headed up into the back, into the Kasbah. That place smelled so bad! I don't think they had a toilet anywhere, just the street.

We were looking for women, you understand. And there were plenty of them. And boy, when they saw us, saw sailors back in their area, man, they came out and made all kinds of bargains. We came out the front way and ran right into the shore patrol. They asked me, "How did you get in there?" I wouldn't tell them. But they didn't stop us, because we were looking for a prophylactic station! We had to get there real quick!

Divers: I didn't see many brothers in North Africa. Then I saw a brother, but he was a Senegalese in the French army. I walked up and spoke to him. He just looked at me.

Watkins: They were speaking French. He probably thought, "What's he talking about?"

Divers: When I saw he had a different insignia on, I said, "Oh, okay." In Mers el-Kébir we couldn't give the people any food—officially. But the people were so hungry they would come and go through our garbage. The skipper decided we could give them a treat. So we washed the garbage cans out and put all the food in there and set it on the shore. After the first time, the people knew. They were lined up, and they knew what time it was coming and everything. We had at least three cans, and we did it every day. The skipper said, "Well, we're not supposed to give it to them, but I didn't say you couldn't put it out there." They were *starving*.

Watkins: That was Blackford.

During the *Mason*'s return trip to the United States, Germany surrendered. The war with Europe was over.

Graham: Right before the war ended in Europe, and soon after Roosevelt died, Buchanan and I were up on deck. We were on the starboard side looking into the sunset, and I saw that the clouds formed a beautiful vee for victory, with the red-white-and-blue stripes in it. It was a humongous thing there, and I was looking at it. I thought Buchanan had seen it too. So afterwards I said, "Did you see that vee for victory, Skinny?"

"No," he said.

"It was right over there, Skinny. You were looking at it."

"No." And it turned out that I was the only guy that saw it. I asked all the other guys, "Did you see it?" and they said, "No." It was a formation of clouds and the sunset. But there was the red, white, and blue, and it was a definite vee. It had stripes like the flag. Nobody saw it but me! Anybody I asked about it said, "No," and for a long time I didn't even mention it. I mentioned it to Barb and I mentioned it to Buchanan, but we didn't linger on the subject.

Buchanan: I was still hoping to get a U-boat. I thought one might surrender to us. I was practicing my German so I could go aboard, but our voyage home was quiet.

War Diary (11 May 1945): patrolling as before in station #2. At 1400 conducted steering casualty drill and Captain made weekly material inspection. Prize crew further organized and trained for boarding surrendered German submarines.

Buchanan: I went aboard the *Mason* as a signalman striker. We had only four signalmen aboard ship, so on our convoys we had four watches between us. I would work every twelve hours, where the rest of the ship was working every eight hours. In the extra time I had gotten to know the ship pretty well. In fact, I even navigated that ship quite a bit. On our last voyage there was one officer who used to go up there and get an extra nap, and I loved the guy, because he'd just leave me in charge! Keeping the point on the convoy, reading the radar, I knew all of that stuff!

DuFau: We could relax a little bit more on the way home. We didn't know it was our last convoy, but we knew no U-boats were after us, and we could take pleasure in the beauty of the ocean. You like to think about sailors being rough-and-tumble guys, you know, or hard characters. But there was something about the beauty of that ocean, and to see the stars at night and to see the sunset. Some of the roughest guys would stop and admire the beauty that was there. Many of the guys were so filled, inspired. . . . It did something to you to see nature in its raw beauty that way. You would think somebody had painted that picture, to see it all there right before your eyes. It was truly fantastic.

Garrison: The flying fish would come up out of the water and glide, I guess, about ten or fifteen feet. A lot of them would land on deck.

Craig: One of the things I did when I got on board was to make regular paydays every two weeks. Well, this developed into a problem because they got their full pay and then they gambled on board. You know, life on board ship is pretty darn boring. So I went to Blackford and said, "Well, here's the problem, Captain. They don't have anywhere to spend the money. The ship store doesn't carry anything. What they're doing is gambling with it. What I'd like to do is set up five-dollar paydays while we're at sea, give everybody five bucks at that point, and then when we come back to the States, give them full pay and whatever they have accumulated in the meantime." Captain Blackford was reluctant. He thought the men deserved their full pay on time, but he agreed. So we did, and it worked out well.

DuFau: Gambling. Those guys would've found a way to gamble.

Garrison: You could gamble for cigarettes.

Graham: Those guys would play with anything, even with beans. Then they'd catch you on payday.

Garrison: Just as you have professional gamblers in civilian life, you had professional gamblers in the navy, and they could clean you out in five minutes.

Graham: They were very, very rich! De Cuir was so quick, he was just taking money home by the seabag full.

DuFau: De Cuir was sleeping on the top sack one night, and he had his dice stuck in his belt. While he was sleeping he pulled the shirt out, and the dice were laying on his stomach. Somebody saw them, and when they woke up De Cuir, his bunk was surrounded by several guys.

Garrison: His victims.

DuFau: They wanted to know, "What goes?" He took the dice and threw them away and said, "Hey, get out of my face!" You know, he threw them overboard. So I asked him, "De Cuir, what was in your mind when you took them dice and threw them away like that?"

He said, "Man, I was so *scared*. I couldn't think of nothing else to do. Because if I started to jump up to run, they would have torn me to pieces. To see those big guys standing around me, and I'm laying flat on my back, I couldn't do nothin'. They would've known that they were bad."

Graham: You could check the dice. All you had to do was put them together and check them.

DuFau: But the guys who used them, they were so smart that they could shoot the doggone things and get them off the scene. If you were watching the money out there, they would switch the dice, and they were good at it.

Graham: Decuir was a city slicker.

DuFau: But he was good at it.

Garrison: He was from New Orleans!

DuFau: No he wasn't. He wasn't from my hometown.

Garrison: Then from where?

DuFau: Baton Rouge.

There was another character on the ship who was well known to all and about whom there were very mixed emotions. This was Horace, the dog who sailed with them on their convoy duties and almost did not make it home.

Farrell: When we were in Boston we got a call from some woman who had a dog. The dog's name was Horace. It was her son's dog, and he apparently got killed in the war. The dog liked men, and she thought the dog would be happier with a bunch of men on the ship. Well, I thought it was a pretty nutty idea myself, because a ship like the *Mason* is no place to have a dog. It's hard enough for a human being. But Blackford says, "Oh, yeah, I think we ought to take the dog." I got the job of going over and picking up the dog. My wife went with me. This tearful woman delivered the dog to us with a paper sack that contained his favorite food and his bed and a couple of other things. He was going to sea with us.

So I got him in the cab and boy, we hadn't gotten around the block, and I was sorry I had that damn dog. He was all over the cab, and drooling. He was a bulldog, so he was drooling all over me and everything else. I got the damn dog on the ship anyway, and we set sail. The dog *hated* the sea. He would bark at the waves, among other things. If a guy was walking along, he'd snap at him. The guys would be trying to wash down the decks with a fire hose, and he would stand there barkin' and yakkin'. He hated every minute he was on the ship. One guy had to clean up after him; it was pretty messy.

Well, there was one guy, and I don't know who he was (but I wouldn't tell you anyway). He was a bos'n's mate. He really hated this dog more than anything else, and it was his job to keep the decks clean up there. So he was up there hosing down the decks, and here's the dog, yakkin' and yakkin' and yakkin'. It was all this guy could take. Horace was wearing a collar. So he reached down, got the dog by the collar, and as if he were throwing a hammer, he swung around about twice, and over the side went Horace—out in the middle of the Atlantic. Here's this little dog out in the middle of the ocean!

The word finally got out to the bridge that Horace was overboard. We weren't with any other ships or on convoy duty. So Blackford turned this ship around. You know, you don't turn it around in fifty feet when you're going fifteen knots. It takes a long while to make that circle and all. By the time the captain heard about it, and by the time they stopped the ship and got her turned around, we had to be a couple of miles from him.

The whole crew was called out to line the rail. We went back looking for the dog. Son of a gun if we didn't find him. It was hard to get alongside; it was rough. So we came alongside the dog, and here's this little devil swimming toward New York. One of the guys said he was going to go in and get the dog. They tied a line around him, and he jumped overboard. I'm glad a submarine wasn't out there then. They would have really laughed at us. But we had sound gear then; we knew who was around. He jumped overboard, swam out, and got the dog. Then we pulled the guy back to the ship. But the dog was mad, bitin' the guy. He was bitin' the guy all the time they were pullin' him back up on to the ship. Then we turned the ship back toward New York and went on our way.

Buchanan: The time the dog went overboard, I was up on the bridge, and I ran down and changed clothes to get in my swimsuit so I could get over the side. But I was too late. There were about four or five other guys that were faster than me. See, whenever anyone had to go into the water and risk his life (though I never thought it was a risk), there was a kind of ritual that went on right after. You'd come out of that cold water, and the guys that were waiting because they didn't get in the water ahead of you would follow you down into the sick bay. The sick bay was nothing more than a little closet with a Dutch door—and a doctor. Doc Collins was the doctor aboard ship. He was a pharmacist's mate. He'd have that door open, and he'd get out this bottle of whiskey, because the guy that went over the side was going to get him a shot. And we'd stand in the passageway, and all of us would look at him and drool. He'd just look back at us and have his drink! I never got one of those drinks my whole time in the navy! I was too slow!

No matter how the time was passed on board, everyone waited for signs that home was near.

Graham: In the radio shack, we would pick up the signal at fifty miles or longer. We could always turn on the receiver and listen, and we would listen for sounds before we'd get into New York, or wherever we were going. We'd get the music, and then we'd pipe it over the speakers sometimes. I had heard of Nat King Cole for the first time in Boston at a little restaurant they called Sisters. On the jukebox they had him singing "Straighten Up and Fly Right." I liked that. Then I heard "Sweet Lorraine," and I fell in love with that song. I substituted "Sweet Bobbie" for "Sweet Lorraine." I put Barbara's nickname in there. So when we were coming into port, and we could pick up the radio stations maybe ten or twelve miles out to sea, everyone had orders to wake me up if that song should come over the radio. They would come down to the bunk and get me up to come listen to it. "I've just found joy. / I'm as happy as a baby boy / with another brand-new choo-choo toy / when I'm with my sweet Bobbie!"

Garrison: First, we'd get the radio; but another indication was when you'd see birds, land birds. Then you knew you were near land someplace.

DuFau: The PBY Catalina! They used to go quite a ways out to sea on patrol. And when you'd see that plane, that was a good feeling. Of course, being up on the bridge, you had a good idea from the charts that you were close. But it would just make you *feel* better knowing that you were within range.

Watkins: I would use Coney Island to guide us. Coney Island was lit up like a circus, see, and that was home coming in. First, you'd see Coney Island, then you'd see our lady waiting for us. We were always glad to see our girlfriend, the Statue of Liberty. Ooh, man. Back home again!

Divers: Then we'd land at the Brooklyn Navy Yard and put on our dress blues . . .

Watkins: Yeah, we'd be ready.

Divers: Ready to go to town!

War Diary (23 May 1945): patrolling as before as forward picket. . . . MASON closed buoy and began directing traffic. At 0327 the convoy and escorts turned on all navigational lights. At 0345, MASON passed [buoy] "XS" and began sweep up channel. At 0716, Buoy S-11 was reached at which point the local escort was supposed to accept the convoy. No such escort was present accordingly MASON proceeded to visual signaling distance of the Harbor Entrance Control Post at Cape Henry which accepted the convoy at 0855. Immediately the senior officer of the escort detached the escorts to proceed. . . . MASON maneuvered clear of channel, increasing speed to full and at 0950 set course 048 degrees T. for New York. . . . At 2212, the examination vessel was passed and at 2248, MASON passed through the net, proceeding to 35th Street pier.

DuFau: New York was liberty town. New York is known as the best liberty town in the world. There were great clubs, and the Savoy was open at that time too.

On May 27, 1945, Barbara Buchanan and James W. Graham were married. Gordon Buchanan was the best man, and shipmates from the *Mason* were among the guests. Since their ship was docked, the Grahams had a chance to be together during the early days of their marriage. But as happy as their interior world was, the outside world still intruded. Every time Graham had arrived or left the ship, he had faced the animosity that no amount of heroic action in the service of his country seemed to change for him or the crew of the *Mason*.

Graham: We had four ships tied up together, and we were on the outermost side. To get back to the pier we had to cross every one of those ships. There would be off-duty sailors on the ships, and they would all say some derogatory remarks as we passed. "He's from the nigger ship" (or "the black ship") or "Here come the coons." Anything. Same terms that they use today. But we were instructed not to pay them any attention. I'd walk right by them.

I said to myself, "I can't do anything now but get off this ship, and I'll put something on you." I used to fight them all the time. I'd fight them at the drop of a hat if I wasn't on the ship. No one's going to say nothin' derogatory to me and get away with it. I just realized that in the last five years I'm not the guy I used to be; I can't fight!

In the Brooklyn Navy Yard, on Sands Street, I was returning to the ship one night. I got out of the cab, and there was Divers arguing with a guy, a big white guy. And I say, "Divers, what's wrong?"

"This dude agreed to pay half of the taxi fare with me, and I got here, and he don't want to pay it—and he wants to fight."

"You won't fight him. I'll fight him for you," I said. So we got into it.

Roberts: The worst incidence of racism I remember was in Charleston. We were in port, and some USO girls came aboard to dance on the fantail. They were entertaining on each ship. When they came aboard our ship, the white shipyard workers tried to charge up the gangplank and take the girls off. The captain had us man our battle stations, and we turned the guns on them. That stopped it. Really, though, we didn't need the guns. We could have taken them on one by one!

Sometimes opposition from white sailors was so blatant it defied the navy itself.

DuFau: One time in Miami, I think it was, we threw the number-one line over (the one you secure to the pier) and yelled for a seaman to take the line, to heave the line, to pass the line over to the pier. And he stood back and said he wasn't going to take no line off that ship, "off no nigger ship." And the captain told me, "DuFau, as soon as we tie up, keep an eye on that fellow. Go down and get his name and rate and service number." He was just a seaman, so we had to get his service number. I'm sure Blackford saw to it that that guy was dealt with.

The *Mason* had come home from war to find that not enough had changed. The final blow was still to fall. On June 12, 1945, Capt. William Blackford was transferred to Great Lakes Training Station without an explanation. He was also promoted, having received an excellent performance evaluation from his superiors. His family thinks he would have preferred to stay on the *Mason*. Certainly for the crew, Blackford's departure meant the end of their adventure. Their remaining tour of duty was an unpleasant anticlimax.

The Bureau of Naval Personnel's final mention of the *Mason* seems surprisingly curt considering that the whole thrust of the document is meant to answer the question, "Can Negro sailors serve well in the navy?" All it says is, "The USS Mason served in Atlantic convoy duty [and] operated satisfactorily" (92). Perhaps some clue comes in the next sentence: "The creation of additional all-Negro units was contrary to the Bureau's strengthening policy against all-Negro units and at least in part for this reason no additional all-Negro sea-going ships were established" (92). Is it an irony of history that those in the navy who wished to do away with segregation found it within their interest to downplay the achievements of this "all-Negro seagoing ship"? Or is it just that the burden of racist assumptions prevented the navy from seeing evidence of excellence?

One last note about the report. It continually refers to men with less than four years of school as "illiterate." The designation negates the actual level of competence. According to this measure, Abraham Lincoln would be "illiterate." But this use of the word might explain why the *Mason*'s last captain, Norman Meyer, offered to teach his crew how to read and write, in spite of the fact that most of the men had high school degrees and some had graduated from college.

Moored

The *Mason* escorted no more convoys. The crew had expected to go to the Pacific and participate in the invasion of Japan. They could not know that the atomic bombs dropped in August 1945 would end the war. But June became July, and they remained "moored as before," testing ammunition or serving as a school ship for young officers. After Hiroshima the men of the *Mason* just waited for the ship's decommissioning. In many ways the life of the ship had ended when Capt. William Blackford was replaced by Norman Meyer. A member of the Naval Academy's class of 1937, Meyer left the navy after graduation because of eyesight problems. Called back to the service after Pearl Harbor, Meyer served as an onshore staff officer for most of the war.

Lt. James Hair (a member of "The Golden Thirteen"—the navy's first group of commissioned officers) and Ens. Clarence ("John") MacIntosh, two of the navy's first black officers, served briefly on board. While in the navy James Hair spelled his name Hare—"the white way," as he says. Meyer was so proud of his relationship with Hair that he was one of only three nonmembers to contribute his reminiscences to *The Golden Thirteen* (Naval Institute Press, 1993), edited by Paul Stillwell. Meyer also wrote about their time on the *Mason* for the Naval Academy's alumni magazine, *Shipmate* (March 1990).

Unfortunately, Meyer has presented the former captain of the *Mason* and her crew in a most unfavorable manner. He admits to very little knowledge of the ship's record, yet he casually insults the crew and Captain Blackford. For example, on the Albuquerque television show *Outlook New Mexico* that aired in July 1990 on KOB-TV, Meyer called Captain Blackford "a drunken slob" (for which interviewer Marsha Hardeman reproved him). In essence, he says the *Mason* was a "terrible ship" until he, Meyer, shaped it up. "[It] started out on the wrong foot operationally and never quite seemed to set itself right. There had been two tries to pass shakedown trials. It's performance escorting convoys had been undistinguished to say the least." But there is no evidence in the ship's log, the convoy reports in the navy archives, or in any of the recollections of the officers or men to support his negative characterization of the ship before he came aboard.

Meyer himself had little direct experience in convoy duty. He served in only one convoy as an officer on the USS *Saucy*. According to his own account in *The Golden Thirteen,* Meyer had such difficulty relating to the captain and other officers of that ship that he left, telling his wife, "I'm done. I quit. I quit." With the help of a psychiatrist he was able to return to the ship. The doctor observed: "You [Meyer] just set your standards too high. Why don't you come on down to the earth with the rest of us human beings?"

In the interview for this book Meyer seemed unaware of the effect that his remarks—based on what he considers to be widely held, conventional-wisdom judgments of women, African Americans, Catholics, and other minority groups—have on the listener. I did not include those asides, however, choosing to stick to material relevant to the *Mason* story.

After the interview for this book (recorded in October 1993), Meyer wrote in a letter that perhaps he misstated the conditions on the *Mason* so as to inflate his role. "I have been known to exaggerate and/or be in error and you would not want any of that in your book." Indeed, he had apologized to the crew at their 1991 reunion, but he has continued to make statements that besmirch the *Mason* and her crew.

The USS *Mason* Association members are both puzzled and angered. In Meyer's version of events, he was the captain who shaped up a sloppy ship. Yet for them, William Blackford was their only true captain; Meyer was just someone who filled in until decommissioning. At the time, they shrugged off his racist attitudes; prejudice was a fact of life to them. It is hoped that now, however, this book has set the record straight. Interestingly, what the crew remembers most about Captain Meyer is an inability to dock the ship and the times they crashed into other destroyer escorts.

Norman Meyer: An officer that I knew had been killed out in the Pacific, so I requested a transfer to the staff in Pearl Harbor. I was on the staff at Pearl Harbor for almost two years in connection with training and evaluating ships before they went out to the battle zone. Well, I am from Minnesota and really had never known Negroes. A few janitors we had in Annapolis, that's all. But I had never seen any talented Negroes.

I heard about the Myrdal book (*An American Dilemma*), and so I sent away for it. And when I read it, the complete story about Negroes and how they were treated, I was incensed and outraged. I said, "This is *terrible* that citizens would be so badly treated." One person could not do much, but I was going to do that.

So I wrote to the Navy Department and said, "I hear you have ships with Negro crews. And if you're looking for a skipper for one"—knowing that it probably was not an attractive post.

They came back and said, "We have one, and the reputation is, it's a terrible ship"—the professional reputation.

I said, "Well, I am now a Reservist. My reputation is back at a factory in New Jersey where I now work. I'll take it."

When asked on what he based his assessment of the *Mason*'s reputation, Meyer made the following reply: "Well, I didn't know anything myself. The people in the Navy Department who assigned officers and so on merely told me that. And I didn't make an investigation of it. I had enough confidence in my own ability that if it was a ship with problems, I figured I could manage those."

Farrell: A terrible ship? Baloney!

Craig: I don't understand Meyer. Meyer, of course, was an academy graduate. He was a bit of a martinet, and he tried to sort of assert his authority in a way that Blackford never had. He had been a staff officer out in Hawaii, I think, before he came to us. He had left the navy after he had graduated from the academy because he had eyesight problems, I think. But then when the war came along, he was brought back in. And I always thought he was a hard guy to get along with.

Divers: He [Meyer] announced he was going to teach reading and writing to us. Here was the cream of the crop of all the black sailors. Now, we weren't dummies. When the navy picked us, they went through all of our service records and our test scores and all of that stuff. And he's going to teach us how to read and write! That's how ill informed he was about what he was in command of.

Meyer: When I was ordered to report to the *Mason,* I was going to get literacy material to teach reading and writing. I quickly saw that that was not necessary. It was a picked crew of outstanding men.

Watkins: Boy, I couldn't like him. He was something. First thing he did was to run the ship into another ship.

Deck Log (14 June 1945): 16–20 Moored as before. At 1552, all tests completed, underway from NAD, Earle, N.J. to Pier #42, North River, Manhattan Is, N.Y. with assistance of a tug. Steering courses and making speeds to facilitate navigation of channels. . . . At 1825 fantail collided with fantail of DE-577 due to set of ebb tide. Minor damage to two starboard chocks, four depth charge arbors bent. The DE-577 sustained a hole, well above the water line in her steering engine room port side aft. No evidences of further damage.

Craig: The chief thing, of course, when you're handling the ship, is bringing it into port and exiting out. And Meyer knew nothing about that. He just couldn't do that because he had been a staff guy. And Blackford knew boats. He'd say, "Oh, it handles like a Buick." But Meyer just couldn't handle the ship. In New York harbor Meyer tore a hole in the ship that we were tying up alongside of. We were up at about 35th Street, and we were tying up alongside of another DE. Meyer just didn't take into account the current as he pulled in, and the ship, of course, then started to go downstream. We had these K-guns on the side— the K-gun was a way of discharging a depth charge. These things had steel brackets that extended out a few inches behind the hull of the ship. One of those just cut a hole right in the ship that we were to tie up alongside of. Now, he would have been in serious trouble but for the fact that the captain of the port was a classmate of his at Annapolis and sort of brushed over it.

Meyer: Well, what happened was, we went out exercising. Because the minute I took command, I took the ship out into New York harbor and drill-drill-drill-drill-drill to get them up to what I thought was . . . One day we came back in, and of course, a lot of the guys had their girlfriends and wives there, and they were anxious and I was anxious to get ashore. And the pilot was very slow. So finally I said, "Well, I'm pretty good at handling a ship; I'll take it in." And here was this slip, you know. So we started in, but what I didn't realize is that the minute the bow of the ship gets in here, to the still waters, the stern is still out in the fast current, and it's twisted like that. And it banged into the dock, or the ship next to us, and cut a hole about a foot square into it.

So the next day, I had to go down to the office. The officer in charge there had been one of my mechanical drawing professors at the Naval Academy. He was a short fella. Now short fellas don't like tall fellas, and I was tall. So he really gives me a talking to. "You should have waited" and this, that, and so on, and "I'll have to report this to the Navy Department."

"Yes, Captain," I'd say, or "No, Captain," you know. He was really giving it to me. And finally I said, "Good-bye, Captain."

As I got to the door, he said, "I'm not going to do it, but don't do it again, Meyer."

Deck Log (16 June 1945): 08–12 Moored as before. 0815 Y068 with Mr. MC ELOVRY at conn came alongside and collided on port quarter. Damaged port depth charge rack and dished in hull at frame 160 about two inches over an area of approximately one foot. 1000–The Commanding Officer held personnel inspection. 1045–Secured from Captain's inspection.

Divers: Well, he [Meyer] sort of looked down on us, treated us like we weren't quite ready for what we were doing. Oh, let's see. How can I say that? That he had to put up with us, you know, and that he was doing us a favor by being there, and he was going to look after us. When actually, we had already been looked after. The war was over. We'd done our duty.

Meyer: In that two years that I had been at Pearl Harbor, I would go out on board a battleship cruiser or destroyer, and within five minutes of looking around I could tell whether the ship could shoot. I developed that sense of evaluation. When I walked on board the *Mason*, I could see that it didn't perform well. It got along, but it just wasn't a real top-notch ship. For example, when it's time to get under way, the exec will say to the captain, "Captain, the ship is ready to get under way." And it is. It wasn't so on the *Mason*. There was always some rope tied to the dock, or somebody hadn't completed some routine. It was just poor organization.

Divers: It's peacetime hokum. And why he would get so much publicity and so much ink on it is beyond my understanding.

Meyer: The problem had been one of leadership. They reflected their boss (Captain Blackford) and the standards that the boss set. We're all sort of innately lazy, and if we're permitted to get away with being lazy, we're lazy.

Within the first couple of months, I had three men who were discharged from the navy for bad conduct. For instance, one of them came up to me, and I saw that he had a long list of offenses—Captain's Mast. So I said, "I see you've got all of this. If you come up here again, I am not going to do anything. You are going to discharge yourself from the navy."

"Oh," he says, "Captain, don't you worry. I'm not coming up here again."

Three weeks later, he was there. And I said, "Johnny, remember you were here three weeks ago?"

"Yes."

"Remember what I said?"

"Yes."

"Well, you just did it. You just kicked yourself out of the navy."

Craig: He demoted the executive officer, Ed Ross, and in effect took his job away from him, although he was the senior officer next to Blackford when Meyer arrived. Ross was a lieutenant.

We had a good crew, and we had an experienced bunch of officers who had been with the ship since she had been commissioned, back in the spring, I guess, of '43. He made Phillips his executive officer. Phillips was rather friendly to Meyer. He tended to be a little bit more of a disciplinarian than some of the other guys. He had been the communications officer.

Meyer: I got a new executive officer, and I got rid of another officer. I had invited one officer after another down to my cabin for a cup of coffee to talk. Well, a couple of them just told me nothing. But the third officer, John Phillips, just exploded, and told me about some troubles that were partly a reflection on the earlier captain. So I made him exec.

Lieutenant Anderson, the engineering officer, was *superb*. And as a result, the engineering gang was superb. The communications officer was so-so, and as a result we had lousy communicators. You know, it comes down to leadership. The men reflect their leaders just like a mirror. I was trying to do what I could for better relations between whites and Negroes. There was a stereotype that Negroes had lots of body odor. And it wasn't true. So I said to John, "I think you and I should write an article for *The Saturday Evening Post* stating that it isn't true about body odor with Negroes."

"Norm," he says, "you're gonna write an article about body odor? You fool!"

Farrell: I was the engineering officer. There was no officer named Anderson in the E section.

Meyer: I very much wanted to have a black officer on board—at least one, or maybe more. One day, the *Mason* was going into a dock in New Jersey near Sandy Hook, and a tug helped us come in, which was normal. I looked down, and that ship just sparkled. Just in *every* way: the way it performed and its cleanliness and so on. And I looked, and as far as I could see, everyone on board was black. Actually, that's not true, but the skipper, indeed, was black. So I quickly invited him over for lunch, and his crew was very happy that their very outstanding skipper, Jim Hair, who had been an enlisted man on a tug before he went to training, was being invited over to have lunch with a superior, or with a senior officer.

And I had the Myrdal book under my arm, and we talked a lot about it. And when he got back to his ship, everybody said, "What happened, Captain? What happened?" I immediately called Washington, and I said, "I want Jim Hair transferred to my ship." And then his crew was very unhappy, because they loved Jim Hair, he was such a good officer. But Jim came on board. And immediately he and I bonded as . . . had the same feelings, the same standards, the same concerns, and were absolutely open. He was not Negro and me white; we were two officers.

And he was a tremendous . . . He was a catalyst, you see. No matter what my feelings might have been towards Negroes . . . Undoubtedly, some of them sort of wondered, "What's this honky Meyer up to?" whereas Jim could interpret me to the crew.

One thing I never really understood was how patriotic the blacks were. Their attitude was very openly, "This is my country and I want to fight for it." I used to ask Jim, "How can you be so damned patriotic when you saw your own brother-in-law lynched in front of you?"

Jim would just reply, "You have to go on living."

James Hair: Moving to the *Mason* was another one of those cases of mixed feelings. I was going to a bigger ship, one that was part of the fighting Navy, but I was sorry to lose the satisfaction of having my own command. I know the men of the tugboat were sorry to see me go, and I felt a sense of regret about that, but they realized this was a step upward. On board the *Mason*, the enlisted crew was all black, and the officers were all white until I got there. I was the first lieutenant, in charge of all deck operations and the topside appearance of the ship. Everything had to be shipshape, including the boats, the hatches, portholes, rigging, anchors, and so forth. We had a very fine crew in the destroyer escort, although I have to admit that there wasn't as much closeness and feeling of family as there had been in the tugboat. That's one of the things you lose when you go to a larger ship (taken from *The Golden Thirteen*, pp. 232, 234).

Divers: But the reason he [Meyer] got Hair was because he needed somebody to run the boat. Hair was the skipper of a tugboat, and this guy Meyer had never run a boat.

Watkins: That's right.

Divers: He was running other ships over, he couldn't dock a ship. That's why he got Hair. When he found out Hair could dock a ship or handle a ship pretty good, that's why he got him. That's my opinion, anyhow. In fact, I didn't know Hair was black until I saw that discharge. I didn't know Hair was a black guy; I always thought he was white. He didn't tell anybody. He appeared white. I mean, if he was black, he sure didn't let anybody know. It didn't get out among the general population. I never held it against him, though. He's still all right. I met him at the reunion.

Watkins: He was all right. He paid for all the cab fares. Nice fellow.

War Diary (8–17 July 1945): Undergoing refresher training as scheduled by ComDesLant. All exercises conducted in Casco Bay operating areas, following schedule conducted underway:

11 July 1945: Ship handling and general drills.
12 July 1945: Tactical maneuvers, towing breeches buoy, visit and search, underway damage control.

13 July 1945:   ASW.

16 July 1945:   AA firing, damage control, night illumination.

Meyer: One of the first jobs we did was to test four hundred sonic depth charges, which would be set off by the sound of the screws of the submarine. But if we dropped them off ours, and our own screws set them off, we'd blow ourselves up—and I wouldn't be here. And these were big, heavy, three hundred-pound depth charges: two hundred one day, then we went back and reloaded, and two hundred the next day. First off, I thought, "Gee, this is great. They're giving us immediately a chance to show how good we are," which we were. But then I said, "Maybe they figure, 'That damn nigger ship isn't worth anything; let it blow up and we haven't lost anything.'" But we got a letter of commendation of how . . . what a good performance we had done. And we were pretty proud and happy about it.

James Hair left the ship on July 21 and returned four weeks later. Norman Meyer would leave on September 20, turning command over to John Phillips. So Meyer spent only six weeks with Hair.

Meyer: At Fort Lauderdale we were having a contest with the submarine during the day, and then at night we'd tie up. Every time when I went to a southern port, I would go to the police and I would say, "This ship is here. We've got a whole lot of black people. They are not steward's mates, they are not cooks and stuff, no more than one or two. They are people that have been out here fighting the war for you, and I expect them to be treated with respect."

Well, this one time, at 2:00 A.M., they called me. "Captain, Captain, the police got Willie, and they're gonna lynch him." So I got down to the police station, and sure enough, they had Willie. It turns out eight of the buddies had gotten in a cab and come through from black town to white town. Going through the white town, the police said Willie had yelled at this white woman, at two o'clock in the morning. But Willie was so scared he could hardly breathe, much less . . . Anyhow, what sort of a woman is walking down the street alone at 2:00 A.M.? So I got Willie back to the ship because, as I told the police, "You know,

I was here yesterday and told you I wouldn't stand for this," and I stood up for the crew's being treated with respect.

The next day, though, I got the crew together and I said, "This happened, it's wrong, but we're down South and we're going to have to live within this context. And furthermore," I said, "if we do have an incident, I'll restrict all of you to the ship." I think that's the day they gave me the nickname of being "The Warden," which is not a term of endearment amongst black people.

War Diary (22–27 July 1945): Operating with other ships of TG 28.4. ASW and counter measures conducted 22, 23, 25, 27 July. Total time 19 hours operating with submerged sub.

War Diary (August 1945): Conducted Training Cruises as follows: (In Miami except when underway)

(a) 2 August: Off Miami for AA Gunnery.
(b) 3, 4 August: PT Vectoring exercises off Miami.
(c) 6–11, 13–15, and 17 August: Underway in area from Miami to Dry Tortugas carrying out scheduled officer training.

Craig: Ross was the navigator as well as the deck officer. He certainly knew how to bring the ship in. But when we went into Bermuda one time, Meyer was on the bridge, and we damn near ran into a shoal. I was standing on the lower part of the ship with Ross, and he said, "See you in a minute," and he went running up to the bridge and warned the captain that he was going off course. He happened to be familiar with the Bermuda harbor because he'd been there before.

Meyer: A certain submarine had been developing evasive tactics to avoid the Japanese surface ships. But they wanted a ship that had never experienced that so they could scrimmage, like a football team. So they designated us. The first day, the submarine was ten miles away, restricted and so on, and we were to find it. Well, Monday we found it. Friday of that week was graduation day, and they could practically do anything they wanted to evade us. Of course, in order not to waste time, if the sonar operator got a contact, he would say "Contact," and I would say "Bearing," back and forth. The sonar team was superb, just superb! One fellow was sounding out Beep, Beep, Beep, Beep-*Beep*, and instead of saying "Contact," he said, "Who dat?" Heh. Heh. But I knew what he meant.

Also, I thought that going around with shirttails out looked sloppy and unmilitary. So I'd go around with the scissors and cut the shirttails off square.

Divers: Captain Meyer was never in a situation where he could prove his leadership because it was all peacetime when he came in. It was all back to the peacetime navy. He kind of reminds me of Captain Queeg from *The Caine Mutiny.* Shirttails, what nit-picking. The *Mason* had always passed inspection. I know because I used to log it. I've never known one time for us to come up short. We were a DE. We'd been at war.

Meyer: They were in charge of playing records, music over the P.A. system. And I had to pass a rule that they couldn't play one record, any one record, more than ten times in a day, otherwise they'd play the damn thing thirty times. You could go crazy.

Divers: You've got to remember, we were nineteen-, twenty-, twenty-one-year old guys! You put a bunch of guys like that together, and they've got a song they like, they'll play it over and over and over. They'll play it from now on, if you let 'em. Like the kids nowadays. How many times does the little guy come in here and play a rap song? I say, "Lance, can't you play something else?"

"I like it, I like it!"

"Don't you ever get tired of it?"

"No! No!" That's the way we were. We had Dinah Washington with Lionel Hampton. She used to sing "The Old Salty Papa Blues."

Buchanan: "I'll Walk Alone," that was the song I loved. Anybody who was in the war remembers that song. I played it because it made me feel good. It helped the other guys too. We even used to dance together sometimes on the fantail. Good thing Captain Meyer never saw *that.*

Meyer: Way at the end, we were at the Charleston Navy Yard for decommissioning. I said, "Jim [Hair] and John [MacIntosh], I want to take you to the Officers Club and have a drink."

"Well, Captain," they said, "we want to go to the Officers Club, but we don't want to go with you."

"What the hell is this? Reverse discrimination? You want to go but you don't want . . ."

"No, no," they said. "The reason we don't want to go is we know that you're going to get in trouble if you take us there, and we don't want you to get in trouble." Which I guess you

might say is an evidence of the affection that Jim felt for me—
and vice versa.

So we went to the most conspicuous place in the Officers
Club and ordered a drink. Service almost stopped because all
the help—the cooks and so on—were black. We could see the
guys looking around the corner. "My God, what is this? A black
officer in our club?" So we had our drink, and then Jim Hair
said, "Well, Captain, you had your fun. Can we now go to black
town and relax with our people?" And that was that.

But the division commander was in a different part of the
club, and when he saw me, he said, "That was a goddamn stupid
thing for you to do." People didn't take blacks to an Officers
Club.

Hair: I know that Norman Meyer has told you about the time he
took me and John MacIntosh to the Officers' Club for dinner. It
was an uncomfortable situation, but Commander Meyer's
presence kept us from getting any direct heat. On the other hand,
if we had gone there without him, just the two of us, the whole
thing might have been okay because it would have been less
ostentatious. He was deliberately putting us on display. He
strongly believed in doing the right thing, no matter what the
consequences were (taken from *The Golden Thirteen*, p. 234).

Watkins: There was the story about Meyer taking Hair to the
Officers Club, where they didn't want him.

Divers: A lot of times you don't like being first.

Watkins: That's right.

Divers: Yeah, you can get your ass whipped being first. Or die. Let
somebody else be first. That's what I used to say all the time! Why
would Meyer want to take Hair there with all them rednecks? The
rednecks would be down there, and they'd get half full of that
beer and start whoopin' and whoopin' and hollerin' that rebel
yell. That's the *last* place you'd want to be! I'd say, "I'll pass this
time."

Watkins: Really.

Divers: I don't ever want to be first. I'll be second.

I certainly wish I could have seen Captain Blackford after
the war, but he died in 1970, before we started having reunions.
You know, gotten together with him, had a reunion with the
guy. He was a marvelous guy. And I thought many a time that
I wished I could have seen him and thanked him for seeing us

through. I went all through the war without a scratch, and I think a lot of that was his doing. A whole lot of it was his doing, his handling of the ship. And I'm quite sure that Skipper Meyer couldn't have done a fabulous job like Skipper Blackford did.

DuFau: We had already had six trips overseas, convoy duty with submarines, and after all that, he [Meyer] came aboard to teach us how to do it right! It was such an insult to us. Meyer *insists* that he is right. Yet, he apologized to us. But then he turned around and made the same statements again, degrading us!

Garrison: He [Meyer] implied that Lieutenant Hair was the one who was needed to bring us in line.

DuFau: [Meyer] said that Hair was the catalyst. We didn't even know him. He just came aboard when Meyer came aboard, and Hair wouldn't have been aboard if Meyer didn't *need* him, need to learn from Hair.

Aweigh

The war ended. The navy offered the crewmen of the *Mason* a chance to stay on, but the highest rank they could aspire to was that of petty officer in a navy that was still segregated. The lack of opportunity kept some from pursuing a naval career. Others just wanted to get out.

Grant: I wouldn't have stayed even if they had made me an admiral. I was ready to go home.

Buchanan: Oh, I was ready to stay! I was ready to stay in the navy. But I was afraid that I was going to get shipped to Norfolk. That's where I got sick. That's where I spent thirty days in the hospital for scarlet fever. *No way* would you get me back there. And I only needed a half-credit more to get out of the navy. I told them no. I went in and saw the officer and said, "Look, I think I'm sick," and they sent me down to sick bay.

"Nothing wrong with you," they told me.

I said, "I know, but man, all I need is half-a-point and I'm out. I'm out. I'm *dying* to get out now, because I know that my name is on the list to go to Norfolk." Norfolk! The hellhole of the navy on the East Coast. I wasn't going back there, no kind of way. I had been in the different southern ports. I found out how I was going to be treated.

Now, I was already a second-class petty officer. They were going to give me first-class petty officer, and I would have been very happy with that if there was some place I could stay. But not Norfolk. No way. After I came out I became a New York City policeman. I did a lot of undercover work. I was shot while on duty and had to retire.

In the last years I've gone back to school to study liberal arts: art courses, ancient history, Egypt. I was studying all this, and I realized I didn't know anything about the Jews. NYU had a course about the history of the Jews. Not only did I grab the course, I started learning Yiddish and Hebrew. I got into Hebrew so good that I wanted to read the Bible in Hebrew.

Lately, I've been working with my sister and brother-in-law on the *Mason* history. I got out my old diary, but I kept notes in here [taps head]. I would draw everything. Anything I would find, I'd draw it and see for myself. I wrote down places I was, things we did. We found all of it confirmed in the navy records down in the Washington, D.C., archives.

I have a couple of poems in my diary that I like too. There's one poem by Powell, who dedicated it to "A helluva fella and friend." I won't let this book out of my hands. I *don't* let it out of my hands.

DuFau: It was a wonderful relationship aboard ship. We really developed a family, and that feeling still exists. When I'm among these guys now, the memories come out. We relive those moments. Every time we talk, we come up with new stories, new incidents that happened way back when. And we have to be so cautious now, because when we're talking and our wives are around, we may say something and be in trouble about it later on trying to explain. If the women get to mumblin' at you, you're in bad trouble.

There were problems, but we just couldn't fight hate with hate. That wasn't our role there, to fight hate. We were there to prove ourselves. Nowadays, you see so many black officers. To think that we were part of that beginning . . . it's wonderful to know that I played a small role in giving others an opportunity. I have the dream of *all* Americans together. You're still *American*, under one flag, under God, with liberty and justice for all. And I believe that. I may be called stupid or something like that, but I still believe it. That was *embedded* in me. From my school days on, I never had anyone preach hatred, told me anything about trying to hate. I was always taught to love and respect others. Love and respect yourself first, then respect others. It's so simple. It would solve so many problems.

I had the opportunity to show that I was as American as anybody! I don't take a backseat to anybody being American. You do what you can, wherever you are, to make this nation work. I felt that I owed it to the nation to take part in defending the flag. That flag still means a lot to me. I still like to hear our national anthem. I still like to sing it. I don't take a backseat to anybody. The president is no more American than *me*. I don't appreciate people bringing their hatreds here and wanting to practice them and still calling themselves Americans.

Be real. Don't be singing the anthem and then go out and kick somebody around because their skin is a different color.

Civilian life didn't offer me an opportunity to practice anything I had learned being a signalman in the navy. But having a wife and a kid, I had to get busy as fast as I could. I just wanted to be working. I had to take all kinds of little menial jobs until, eventually, I went into construction work, and I was in that for about twenty-six years. I got my benefits and everything from construction work. It was a very interesting role to play in New York. I can see buildings where I mixed mortar to go between the bricks to help build them. That's a contribution, and I was a part of it. I am *very* happy about being a part of making something constructive, making something beautiful.

And the same thing in everyday life. If I can say or *do* something for someone to lift up somebody's spirits, I will do it. I carry out here in everyday life the closeness that existed among the navy crew. I strive to keep that calm atmosphere around me, do what I can to solve any problem that I'm around.

Graham: I went to so many trade schools, it wasn't even funny. And I went to Delahanty Radio and Television, FM and Television, technician this and technician that. I went to RCA Engineering School for about six weeks. But what's the use? I must have looked for years for a job. I just couldn't get a job. And I went to one that was advertised in an electronics publication. The name of the place was on 72nd Street and York Avenue. I was sure this guy was going to give me a job as an electronics technician. He put me to work sweeping up—that sort of thing.

Eventually, I got a job. I couldn't get a job in what I wanted, so I started repairing television sets. I stayed with that until the time I retired in '86. It was good money. In those days I was making sixty dollars a week and living high on the hog. I was the only guy on the block with a new car. I was trading the car in every two years. I built my own television set in time for the Joe Louis fight. I had the whole neighborhood lined up on my sun porch.

But I never forgot my experience on the *Mason*. I was part of the navy, and I was very proud to be a sailor. The *Mason* was decommissioned in 1945, and she was sold for scrap in 1947. But there was never anything in any of the newspapers about the *Mason*. I used to watch the documentaries on World War II all the time, and I'd look from beginning to end, and I never saw a black face in them. Once or twice you'd see the black face of a black soldier or a sailor, but most of the documentaries were strictly white.

The *Mason* kind of fell through the cracks and was never heard of after. But there was another ship—not a ship, it was a patrol craft—that also had a black crew, and it seemed that that one . . . they favored that one over ours.

Back in 1973, I think, there was a writer by the name of Gibson. His grandmother was very famous; she was the Gibson Girl. He wrote a book about one particular convoy that we took over. There were waves ninety feet high, winds at ninety miles per hour. He wrote a book about that particular convoy, NY-119, and he had a book party down at the South Street Seaport Museum.

The author had a whole piece in his book about the *Mason*, and I met a lot of the guys at the book party who had served in the navy at that time. Through one man I enlisted in the Destroyer Escort Sailors Association (DESA). We had a little bimonthly paper I used to look at religiously to see if I could find some of my shipmates listed or something about the *Mason*. There was never anything. Then Dr. Martin Davis decided that he would organize a branch of DESA here on Long Island, and we named it SOL DESA—Statue of Liberty DESA. The night that we were supposed to meet was a very bad, snowy night, and we didn't meet. Dr. Martin called me the next day on the telephone, and we started talking. I mentioned the *Mason* and the black sailors. He had never heard of the ship. He said, "Are you sure?"

I said, "Yes."

"That's a shame, because it should be in the history books. Well, I'll do everything in my power to get it in the history books." And from then on, he and I worked together.

I started writing the archives for pictures and documents and a muster of the fellows from the ship. I sent a lot of letters down to St. Louis, to the archives down there, for the history of the ship and so forth. DuFau always lived here in New York, so we contacted him. And from then on, we've been sailing pretty good.

I was determined that it would come to pass. I said I would devote the rest of my life to making sure that it did.

When we first started out, Buchanan was into photography. He taught my wife and me. We'd go over once a week to redo the old pictures, reproduce the old pictures. We made about ten or twelve albums with about 130 pictures each. And we sent albums to Divers, Bland, Garrison, DuFau, among others.

I just decided that I would devote the rest of my life to bringing the *Mason* to the forefront, so that everyone would know about our ship. Because it would be a crime for us to pass through history without our children or grandchildren ever knowing about the *Mason*.

Divers: Until this day, nobody—very few people—knew about the accomplishments of the *Mason*. The story was buried in the archives, in my opinion. It was buried in the archives, and the people that did that are probably all dead. And it's still dead in the bureaucracy. But we've been fortunate lately to be able to dig out a lot of that stuff and fight our case.

The people should know what we did, what we were a success at. Even though they had programmed us to fail, we were very, very successful. Our success made progress possible in all branches of the armed forces. We were capable of doing everything that the rest of the general public was able to do. I feel proud that we were one of the teams in the forefront. We have to fight, fight, fight to bring that out. Us guys are getting up to . . . we're in our seventies now, and even our eighties. We've got to hurry up and get the story out! Otherwise, it will be buried. If we don't do this ourselves, it will never come out.

DuFau: You know, we wanted to be something. We always wanted to have our history recorded. And now we are covering it. We've closed the gap from 1943. Here it is, 1993, and we can stand and talk with officers. Back then it was such a big thing just to be a seaman striker for a rate other than steward's mate and cook. And recently we went to Annapolis and met all these black officers and midshipmen and women.

It tells us that we were on the right road. Even though we were young, we had this idea of overcoming all these barriers that were in our way to prove that there was nobody more American than us. We had to go through so much hell to *prove* it.

We're fading out. Time is catching up with us. We've handed the torch over to the new generation.

Garrison: I was glad when I was discharged that I didn't go back to the South. I don't think that I could have adjusted to it. Although I had lived in it all my life, I don't think I could have readjusted. In three years, you go from being a boy to a man. The service really matures you quickly.

All of us learned in the service that we can live together in close proximity and not fight. I learned that.

I carried other lessons into my later life: the emphasis on punctuality, on doing your best in anything you try to do. If you didn't do a good job, the navy didn't fool around with you too long. They'd get somebody else. So I continued to try to excel in whatever I did.

I was discharged from the service at the Naval Air Station in Charleston, South Carolina, and my family had moved to Brooklyn, New York. I attended Brooklyn College. I found that hard because the other students seemed so immature. I went to New York University School of Religious Education. I had felt the call to the ministry. I studied there, and I also went to the New York City Department of Corrections as a correction officer. I worked in that capacity for sixteen years. I became disabled with a heart attack, and I was out sick two years. At age fifty-four, I went back to Brooklyn College and got a degree in European history and Afro-American history. I pastored a church in Brooklyn for thirty-three years, and I retired in October 1992.

At the time we were involved on the *Mason*, we weren't aware of the fact that we were making history. We knew we were an experiment, but we were so involved in doing what we were doing that that took precedence over any part about making history. But I loved it. I'm glad I did take a part in it. Sometimes it seems almost unbelievable, but it's true.

Gordon: I got married in August of '45, after the war ended. Much of what happened until December the twenty-third, when I got discharged, was a blur because of my being a newlywed. I was out of the navy for four years, then the Korean War started building up. I knew that we were going to get drafted back into the military. I decided, instead of waiting until I got drafted, I would go back in voluntarily for a career and see how many stripes I could get on my arm before the war started.

On the first of December, 1949, I rejoined the navy. I went to aviation and electronics school and became an aviation electronics technician. In the ensuing ten years, I served on various carriers. I taught airborne and radar controlling. I was one of the few enlisted men in the navy to be an airborne controller. I taught navy and air force officers airborne controlling so that they could qualify for their air observer wings.

During the Korean War the navy was not segregated. I was accepted as just another sailor. I still had the mistreatment because of who I was, but I was not lumped into a segregated group any more.

I went up in rank very fast and became a chief petty officer. I tried to get a commission; I applied for a commission. I tried every program they had. I was tops in my field, and there was no reason why I shouldn't get a commission. I could not have made my recommendations any higher if I'd have written them myself, but I never could break into the commission ranks. It seemed to get stopped in the bureau somewhere. I always imagined that it was stopped because of the red lettering on the front cover of my service jacket that spelled out NEGRO.

Peters: The navy has a good way of covering things up that they don't want the general public to know. Look at the events aboard the USS *Iowa*. Remember when that turret exploded? They said a gay sailor committed suicide! The navy tried to cover that up, but then they finally had to come forward and say that they were completely wrong, and the person that they accused has been exonerated. I think the importance of the *Mason* in terms of the history of this country is something that the navy decided they just didn't want out.

I think possibly because it would be giving too much credit to people who were considered at the time not to have 100 percent citizenship. Possibly they did not want to give credit where credit was due.

It's like other omissions of history that eventually come out after years and years and years. But we're talking about fifty years of information that should have come out, or should have been a part of our ongoing history. It's just coming out now, in the twilight of the lives of the people who participated in it. Some of these people will never know that this information ever came out. In some respects, it's devastating. When you think about the amount of sacrifice that you put out on behalf of your country, and that country disregards it, discounts it. That certainly doesn't make you feel good.

Plus, if the story had been known, things might have been different. The integration of the armed forces probably would have occurred much earlier than it did. The USS *Mason* was an experiment. At the time that we were doing this, we were all kids. I never gave any real thought to the fact that this was history. This was something that the country needed, and we were there to give the country what it needed.

I think the officer corps in all of the services would have been more representative of the population of the country. And I think it may have been a catalyst for what took place in the 1960s in terms of the civil rights of black Americans.

I have been a member of the Coast Guard Auxiliary for fifteen, over fifteen years. Both my wife and I do a lot of work for the Coast Guard. And I have a real soft spot in my heart for the Coast Guard. We do a lot of search and rescue work, a lot of public education work—and it's appreciated.

Watkins: There's a Black Sailors Association here in Chicago. I went to a ceremony at the Daley Center once, and one of the members asked, "You're from the *Mason?*"

"Yes."

"Hey, what's your name?" I told him. He said, "Sit on the stage with me," and I did. Then he said, "Oh, you're on next."

"I am?" I don't even remember what I said, but I spoke and they clapped. It's nice to be honored. It's nice.

Graham: One really strange thing—I was watching a documentary about a U.S. pilot who shot down a lot of Japanese planes. He had all these Zeros painted on the side of his plane. I was thinking about how much I'd wanted to paint a U-boat kill on our stack. Suddenly, I realized I was *glad* we never sank a sub. Glad. I would have been an old man at fifty if I had. I would have kept picturing those guys as they went down. Their faces—knowing they were going to die. In war you think "sub," not people, not other men. So I'm glad I didn't kill anybody.

Epilogue

Their story has begun to be told. The Cable News Network sent a producer and cameraman on a ferry to Governor's Island to cover the 1993 reunion of the USS *Mason* crew. Irish Night was the theme of the banquet on Saturday, June 18. Mayor David Dinkins sent a note of congratulations and mentioned that he too had experienced the kindness of Irish people. The *Mason* story reached a national audience, and the reaction to it came first from the crew's relatives. James Graham received calls from nephews in North Carolina, in Virginia, in Florida. Lorenzo DuFau heard from New Orleans. Benjamin Garrison took calls from grandchildren and great-grandchildren.

When a small portion of the *Mason* story was told on the Chicago PBS station as part of *Home Away from Home: The Yanks in Ireland*, I too had heard from relatives. They had enjoyed the entire documentary about the U.S. involvement in the north of Ireland during World War II, but the interviews with the men of the *Mason* had struck a particular cord. The day after *Yanks in Ireland* aired, my cousin called me with the story of his experience in a bar on 103rd Street on the far south side of Chicago. Most of the patrons of this tavern were veterans of Viet Nam whose fathers had fought in World War II. Because many of them were Irish American, they expressed a certain pride in the lack of prejudice the Irish had shown during the ship's trip to Belfast. "An odd kind of self-congratulations, considering the attitudes I'd heard expressed there about black people," my cousin remarked. "But there was something else too. A sympathy for what it's like to serve and have your service ignored. They were rooting for the crew of the USS *Mason* in that bar."

What happened that night in the bar my cousin visited is really the epilogue to the story of the USS *Mason*. The Viet Nam veterans' sympathy for the crew is a good sign of changing attitudes. The crew of the *Mason* went on to live rich lives and made a difference to many people. But when I asked James Graham, Lorenzo DuFau, Benjamin Garrison, and Gordon Buchanan if they felt they had been able to really make the contribution to society that their time on the *Mason* had equipped them for, all of them answered, "No." To think of James Graham being turned away from job after job as other men with less training were hired is to confront white America's problem. He refused to let anger turn his life sour, but he never compromised his dignity. Graham recalls meeting a white sailor years later that he had known in the war. Someone made a racist remark that Graham objected to—verbally. "You're lucky," the white former shipmate told the man. "When I knew him he would have knocked your block off."

"Patience," Graham says. "I learned patience. Just to keep coming back, whether I was wanted or not, until I accomplished my goal."

He had wanted to belong to the Destroyer Escort Sailors Association as a way of bringing the *Mason*'s history to the fore. "The first dinner Barb and I went to, no one spoke to us. We sat alone," Graham recalls. This year he served as vice chairman of the Statue of Liberty chapter, and the men of the *Mason* plan their reunions so they can participate in the ceremonies on the *Intrepid* commemorating Destroyer Escort Day. Part of the CNN coverage included members of the *Mason* crew placing red carnations in a vase in remembrance of destroyer escort sailors who had been lost at sea.

Among the sixteen thousand DESA members are, no doubt, men who had shouted obscenities at the crew and derided the *Mason* as that "nigger ship," but none of that was evident when the veterans stood together to welcome home the USS *Slater*—the only destroyer escort left afloat in the world. The U.S. Navy had given the *Slater* to the Greek navy, who had renamed her *Aetos* (Eagle). Through the efforts of Dr. Martin Davis and the leadership of DESA, the Greek navy had given the *Slater* to the association, which arranged to tow her to New York. When the ship came into her berth at the USS *Intrepid* Sea-Air-Space Museum, Gordon Buchanan said, "We're all eighteen again."

Barbara Buchanan Graham remembered the last DE she had watched come into port—the USS *Mason*. "They'd been talking so proud about 'My ship, my ship'; I'd expected something the size of the *Queen Mary*, and here came this little sliver of a thing." In June 1993 this last DE was bigger than a battleship. The men of the *Mason* signed on again and joined other DESA members in scraping and painting the decks of the old ship. "The *Mason* crew are my most loyal volunteers," says the *Intrepid*'s curator.

It took fifty years for the *Slater* to come home from war. It took the same half century for the U.S. Navy to fulfill the promise it made to seventeen-year-old James Graham in the recruiter's office in Charleston, South Carolina. "I had been attracted to the traditions of the military, the sense of ceremony. Yet I wasn't really supposed to be part of that tradition. At that time the service didn't think a black man could achieve excellence. Then, in May 1993, we spent that week in Annapolis. That was the best experience I ever had in the armed forces."

Plans for that special week began when Mark Gatlin of the Naval Institute Press contacted Capt. Gene Kendall, head of the Math and Science Department at the United States Naval Academy. Captain Kendall is a leader among the growing number of African American naval officers. He was, he says, a militant when he attended Duke University in the 1960s and found the predominantly white university setting stifling. He dropped out, enlisted in the navy, and came up through the ranks with great distinction. He inspired not only the midshipmen but also the young officers who, with him, formed the Black Officers Association. He arranged for Mr. and Mrs. James Graham and Mr. and Mrs. Lorenzo DuFau to attend the Commissioning Week at the Naval Academy and to be Adm. Thomas Lynch's honored guests at the parade of midshipmen and at the graduation ceremonies. The week before, Captain Kendall had himself been commissioned as captain of the USS *Mount Whitney* (LCC-20) the flagship of Second Fleet in the Atlantic.

On May 25, 1993, the Grahams and the DuFaus took their places in the front row of the reviewing box. Not too far away sat the parents of Brigade Commander Jeff Royal, the graduating midshipman chosen by his teachers and peers to lead the brigade at the final parade. Like James Graham and Lorenzo DuFau, Jeff Royal's father had been a navy enlisted man, and like them he is black.

"Did you ever think we'd get so close to this much gold braid?" Lorenzo DuFau asked Mr. Royal. And now the gold braid was in the family. Midshipman Jeff Royal stood at attention, his saber raised. Firmly and loudly he called out the orders that set the companies marching. One by one they saluted as they passed. Adm. Frank Kelso, then-Chief of Naval Operations, and Admiral Lynch, then-Superintendent of the Naval Academy, returned their salutes. So did James Graham and Lorenzo DuFau. In each group many young black men and women marched with their white classmates.

"Our children," Terry DuFau said. "All our children."

"I shook hands with Admiral Lynch and Admiral Kelso," Graham said. "You can tell a lot from a handshake. They were sincerely glad we were there. Sincere. The handshake said a lot. Then Admiral Lynch invited us to his house for a reception afterward. 'You will be there,' he said. And he gave us directions, told us how to get there, so I knew he meant it."

At the reception the Grahams, the DuFaus, and James Graham's nephews, navy men too, visited with the graduates, their families, and many admirals. Graham discovered that Admiral Kelso's wife came from Florence, South Carolina, very near Lake City. A band played, champagne and a cold buffet were served under tents. The sun shone. The young men and women dressed in their white uniforms hugged each other and laughed.

At the honors ceremony that followed, the African American midshipmen made many trips to the stage to accept awards for academic excellence and athletic achievement.

A group of juniors sat together watching the ceremony. They noticed the *Mason* group and stopped to say hello. They were members of the Black Students Association and had heard something about the presence of the crew members on campus but did not know much about the history of the ship. Lorenzo DuFau took out his scrapbook and an impromptu lesson began. "We were the first," he said. As he turned the pages and told his stories the midshipmen moved closer. Then one young man looked up and demanded of no one in particular, "Why weren't we told? Why didn't we know about this?!"

"We've come to tell you," Lorenzo DuFau replied. He and Graham promised they would come back and bring other members of the crew with them.

The next morning they joined other proud families in the football stadium. Painted along the sides were the names of famous sea battles. The theme of Senator John McCain's speech was the end of the Cold War and the new opportunities a world at peace could offer the navy. Again, as the graduates went up to receive their diplomas, the new world order at home was evident. No longer was the navy's officer corps a closed white male club.

David Robinson moved up to the side of the stage to photograph his brother Charles, who was graduating. Next to him an African American marine colonel stood with his camera ready. The little boy he used to babysit for was about to be commissioned an officer in the U.S. Marine Corps.

When the new officers sailed their hats into the air, James Graham and Lorenzo DuFau were ready. And so, Terry DuFau and Barbara Graham walked out of the stadium on the arms of their sailors wearing navy caps cocked to one side.

"This is the second greatest day of my life," James Graham burst out. "It ranks right under my wedding day."

Indeed, *Proudly We Served* exists because of that wedding day. James and Barbara Graham are the heart of the USS *Mason* Association, and their devotion to each other and the association members created this story. Proudly We Served—a love story.

Appendix A

The Negro in the Navy, prepared by the Historical Section of the U.S. Bureau of Naval Personnel in 1947, provides a chronicle of the navy's efforts to keep African Americans out of the navy completely, to control numbers, to confine their service to a separate stewards' branch, to restrict even those in the seamen's branch to menial tasks, and finally, to minimize the achievements of the few black men who actually joined the fleet and manned a warship in the Battle of the Atlantic. It is a document that has never been published. Indeed, when Morris MacGregor refers to it in his collection of pertinent naval documents, he describes coming on the report in a dusty old file cabinet in the far corner of an office where it should not have been. He does not include it in his collection, however.

I found it in an out-of-the-way place also. After searching for the report through many official avenues, I came across it on a shelf of oversized books in the Naval Academy's Nimitz Library. The copy is marked "First Draft Narrative," which makes it doubly valuable as a reflection of official unedited navy thinking of the time. The document acknowledges the dissenting voices from within and without that pushed for equal treatment of black citizens willing to sacrifice for their country. The report opens with evidence that "Older Navy men today recall the service of Negroes aboard the larger combatant vessels from the turn of the century through the first World War" (1). It then admits that, following World War I, "enlistment of Negroes seems to have been discontinued by BuNav" and even the messmen's branch was closed. "[I]n practice, only Filipinos were recruited for this branch from about 1919–1922 until December, 1932."

From 1933 on, African Americans could enlist as messmen, but when World War II opened, there were only six rated black men in the regular navy in the seamen's branch, twenty-three who had returned from retirement, and fourteen in the Fleet Reserve (1).

When, in the Selective Service and Training Act of 1940, Congress mandated that "any person, regardless of race or color, between the ages of eighteen and forty-five, shall be afforded an opportunity to volunteer for induction into the land and naval forces of the United States" and that "there shall be no discrimination against any person on account of race or color," the secretary of the navy created a committee that said, more or less, that since no black men had cracked the navy's exclusionary policy, none should be given the opportunity. "Within the limitations of the characteristics of members of certain races, the enlisted personnel of the naval establishment is representative of all the citizens of the United States. Therefore, no corrective measures are necessary" (4).

When the NAACP wired the navy the day after Pearl Harbor asking that, since the navy was now vigorously recruiting men, black men be included, the answer was simply No. What was the navy's reason? The report states it baldly. "Mingling Negroes with whites in the relatively large number of non-rated billets on larger ships would inevitably promote race friction and lowered efficiency" (5).

So, all of the arguments about lack of preparation of black recruits or fear of water, etc., etc., cover the essential reason for holding African American seamen back—white racism. What is the solution to racism, in the opinion of the navy board? Discrimination. "The reasons for discrimination in the United States are rather generally that: (a) the white man will not accept the negro in a position of authority over him; (b) the white man considers that he is of a superior race and will not admit the negro as an equal; and (c) the white man refuses to admit the negro to intimate family relationships leading to marriage. These concepts may not be truly democratic, but it is doubtful if the most ardent lovers of democracy will dispute them, particularly in regard to inter-marriage" (6).

Anger against the naive do-gooders such as Mrs. Roosevelt or Assistant Secretary of the Navy Adlai Stevenson, who had joined the leaders of the black community in using the navy to conduct the fairness provision of the selective service act, is palpable. Democracy becomes almost a dirty word. Yet, the call to defend democracy formed the essence of the recruiting strategy. It is sadly ludicrous to think that while citizens of African American descent rushed to defend their country, in spite of past injustices, the navy was going to deny them full participation because, "I wouldn't want my daughter to marry one." No wonder the reasoned arguments of black intellectuals, the criticism by black newspapers, and the moral outrage of black church leaders did not move the navy.

What did sway them was the consequence of such exclusion. The report quotes a letter that the chairman of the War Manpower Commission wrote to the secretary of the navy on February 17, 1943, to explain why the services must now take in the hundreds of thousands of black men who had answered the call for recruits and been registered but had been kept from active service in order to fill white calls. After a quick nod to the anti-discrimination ban in the selective service act, he writes that the real reason the army and even the navy must open up is that with so many white males in the services, there is "a higher percentage of Negroes in the civilian population. This situation is made more serious because of the geographical concentration of Negroes and because nearly all of the men involved, Negro and white, have been single" (11). This was coupled with the fear that white registrants might sue, for "The probability of this action increases as the single white registrants disappear and husbands and fathers become the current white inductees, while single negro registrants who are physically fit remain uninducted" (12). So the white fears of black men serving with them had to be balanced against white anger that black men were not.

When the navy finally did open up to black sailors, it created a Training and Control Division "to overcome the inertia with which any large organization meets a new and strange problem" (18). Representatives from this division would "ride circuit" and see how the policies formulated would be carried out. There were some general guidelines: one, "that northern Negroes be not detailed to the South"; conversely, that command be given to white officers of southern background. The first glimmer of sense in the report comes when it states that this policy was called into question. It was "imagination, firmness and capacity to deal with people, rather than any specialized background of 'knowing' Negroes" that made for successful relationships between officers and men and created an atmosphere for achievement (23). One such officer reported to the navy board, "A man may be from the north, south, east or west. If his attitude is to do the best possible job he knows how, regardless of what the color of his personnel is, that is the man we want as an officer for our colored SeaBees. We have learned to steer clear of the 'I'm from the South—I know how to handle 'em' variety" (23).

As the report dutifully moves on, the section on "Negro Competence" begins, "Though whites and Negroes of comparable background made comparable records," it spends the next pages comparing all white recruits to all black recruits, even though the bureau acknowledges that some black sailors had only attended school for a few years. Black college graduates volunteered to teach remedial classes for these men two hours per night, five nights a week, and two hours on Saturday. They volunteered for the extra duty, giving up precious off-duty time! Seventy-two percent of their students passed the navy's examination. So, in fact, when gross numbers are used, the percentage of black sailors who qualified for the most advanced training—Class A schools—is 33.14 percent, compared to 40 percent of **all** white recruits.

Appendix B

Following is a copy of what looks like a form letter sent by Captain Blackford. Presumably this is similar to the documents described by Bill Farrell on page 58.

NAVY DEPARTMENT
SUBMARINE CHASER TRAINING CENTER
MIAMI, FLORIDA

From: Lt. Comdr. William Mann BLACKFORD, DV(G), USNR.
To: The Chief of Naval Personnel.
Via: The Commanding Officer.
Subject: USS MASON (DE 529)–Billeting of.

1. Lieutenant (jg) B. BLACKFORD, Detail Officer at S.C.T.C., advised me that the majority of the enlisted crew of the subject vessel will comprise colored personnel. I was further advised that my assignment in the vessel was not mandatory.

2. I consent to and accept this assignment, i.e., to USS MASON (DE-529) after having been advised of the fact that a colored crew will be assigned to the vessel.

Appendix C

USS MASON (DE 529)

Original Statistics

LENGTH OVERALL:	289' 5"
EXTREME BEAM:	35' 1"

STANDARD DISPLACEMENT:
Tons:	1,140
Mean Draft:	8' 3"

DESIGNED SPEED:
Knots:	21

DESIGNED COMPLEMENT:
Officers:	6
Enlisted:	150

ARMAMENT:
Main:	(3) 3"/50
Secondary:	(1) quad 1.1"
	(9) 20 mm
ASW:	(2) DCT
	(8) single DCP
	(1) multiple DCP
	(Hedgehog type)
Tubes:	none

U.S.S. MASON (DE 529)

Commissioning Date
20 March 1944

Next of Kin of Officers

BLACKFORD, William M., Lt. Comdr., D-V(G), USNR–Mrs. Jane G. Blackford (wife), Seattle, Washington.

ROSS, Edward O., Lieutenant, D-V(G), USNR–Mrs. Roxane B. Ross (wife), New York, New York.

BARTON, Leonard F., Lieutenant, D-V(G), USNR–Mrs. Marilyn Jean Barton (wife), St. Louis, Missouri.

DEAN, Charles B., Jr., Lieutenant, D-V(S), USNR–Mr. Charles B. Dean, Sr. (father), Norwood, Massachusetts.

HOLROYD, Roy L., Lieutenant (jg), D-V(S), USNR–Mrs. Gladys I. Holroyd (wife), Princeton, West Virginia.

FARRELL, William H., Lieutenant (jg), E-V(G), USNR–Mrs. Rosella H. Farrell (wife), Chicago, Illinois.

PHILLIPS, John C., Lieutenant (jg), C-V(S), USNR–Mrs. Janet G. S. Phillips (wife), Bala-Cynwyd, Pennsylvania.

KITTS, William W., Ensign, D-V(G), USNR–Mr. William Z. Kitts (father), Sulphur Springs, Texas.

HARRINGTON, Merton V., Ensign, D-V(G), USNR–Mrs. JoAnn Harrington (wife), Mayville, North Dakota.

SCOTT, Frank T., Ensign, USN–Mrs. Alma B. Scott (wife), Norfolk, Virginia.

W. M. BLACKFORD, Lt. Comdr., USNR, Commanding.

ENLISTED MEN (FROM LOG OF THE USS *MASON*)

ACKMAN, Raymond R.	EM1C	V6
ANDERSON, R. S., Jr.	SC2C	V6
APPLEFORD, Lloyd L.	EM1C	V6
ARCENEAUX, Leroy L.	EM1C	V6
AUZENNE, Edward A.	S2C	V6
BAILS, Monroe J.	EM3C	V6S
BATEMAN, George E.	CMOM P	USN
BATTLES, William A.	S2C	V6S
BEGLE, Claude, Jr.	MOMM3C	V6
BELL, Calvin B.	QM2C	V6
BELL, George Jarome	S1 SC	V6S
BENBOW, Charles C.	S2C	V6
BIGHAM, Jonney	S1C	V6
BLAND, William H. III	S1C	V6S
BLANTON, Lewis F., Jr.	QM3C	V6
BOLTON, Wendell T.	S2C	V6
BONNER, Fred M.	RM2C	V6
BOOKER, Leroy	S2C	V6
BORN, Carl Joseph	CQMA	USN
BOULDIN, Carlton M.	S2C	V6S
BOWSER, Russell J., Jr.	S2RDM	V6S
BRIDGES, Zebedee J.	S1C	V6
BROWN, John H.	F2 MOM	V6
BROWN, John I.	S2C	V6
BROWN, Wilbur R.	S2C	V6
BRYANT, Herbert F.	F2 MM	V6S
BRYANT, Zechariah	EM3C	V6
BUCHANAN, Gordon D.	S1C	V6
CADWELL, Horace H.	SoM3C	V6S
CAMPBELL, Roy	S2C	V6S
CASSIDY, John P.	SK1C	V6
CAVE, Angus Lloyd	PHM3	V6S
CLARETT, Stephen C.	GM3C	V6
CLARK, Willie, Jr.	GM2C	V6

CLOTTS, Paul F.	RT2C	V6
COLEMAN, Leonard	S1C	V6
COLLINS, Lorenzo L.	PHM1	V6
COOK, Roy W.	GM3C	V6
COVINGTON, B. F.	S1C	V6
CRESWICK, William H.	CMOM P	USN
CROOMS, William H.	S2C	V6S
CUMMINGS, Leroy	S2C	V6S
DALRYMPLE, Donald L.	SC2C	V6
DAVIES, Henry	COX	V6
DAVIS, Albert A.	GM3C	V6
DAVIS, Clarence L.	SC2C	V6
DAVIS, Eldred Bryan	Y2C	V6
DAVIS, Joseph W., Jr.	S2C	V6
DE CUIR, Manuel B.	CM2C	V6
DENSON, Fred	S1 QM	V6S
DEYO, Howard C., Jr.	COX	V6
DICKERSON, McKinley	S2C	V6S
DIVERS, Charles W.	QM2C	V6
DONALD, Thomas	S1 QM	V6S
DRELL, Warren J.	CRMA	USN
DuFAU, Lorenzo A.	SM2C	V6
DUNN, James A.	S1 SM	IND
DYKE, George D.	F1C	IND
DYSON, Nathaniel O.	EM2C	V6
DYSON, William W.	S2C	V6S
FAURE, Theodore L., Jr.	CMMA	USN
FORD, Jeremiah	S2C	V6S
FORD, Taft	S1C	V6S
FRANCE, William R.	EM2C	V6
GALLOWAY, Richard A.	S2C	V6S
GARRISON, Benjamin G.	S1C	V6
GEORGE, James A.	S2C	V6S
GERAN, Hamp	S2C	V6S
GIBSON, Frank E.	S2RDM	V6S
GOODEN, Royal H.	QM2C	V6
GOODWIN, Harry J.	S2C	V6
GORDON, Arnold	S2C	V6
GRAHAM, James W.	RM2C	V6
GRAHAM, William J.	SM1C	M2

GRANT, Melvin J.	Y3C	V6
GRANT, Richard, Jr.	S1C	V6
GRAY, Morrison	E.S2C	V6S
GRAVES, Augustus W.	MOMM1C	USN
GRAVES, Donald G.	F1C	V65
GUILD, Harry T.	S2C	V6
HALL, Frank W.	BKR3C	V6
HALL, Robert	S2 QM	V6
HAWTHORNE, Elgin	S2C	V6S
HAYES, Albert E.	S1 QM	V6
HENDERSON, V. O., Jr.	RM1C	USN
HILL, Jack	QM3C	V6
HILL, Rupert J., Jr.	S2 CM	V6
HOLLAND, Marion L.	EM1C	USN
HOLMES, Julius	SM2C	V6
HOPKINS, Robert Lee	FC3C	V6S
HOWARD, Thomas H., Jr.	S1 QM	V6
HOWTON, Norman H.	F2 EM	V6
HUBBARD, Richard	EM3C	V6
HUNTER, Andrew D.	S2RDM	V6S
IVY, Walter T.	S2C	IND
JACKSON, Edward M.	STM2C	V6S
JACKSON, Herbert	MOMM3C	V6
JAMES, Junius E.	S1C	V6
JASMINE, Charles S.	WT2C	V6
JOHNSON, C. S., Jr.	S1C	V6
JOHNSON, Cecil A.	S2RDM	V6S
JOHNSON, Etell C.	S1C	V6
JOHNSON, Eugene W.	S1C	V6
JOHNSON, Fred S., Jr.	S2C	V6
JOHNSON, Marion	S2C	V6S
JOHNSON, Raymond P.	EM3C	V6S
JOHNSON, Richard A.	MOMM2C	V6
JOHNSON, Robert	S2C	V6S
JONES, Freddie J.	SF2C	V6
JONES, George L., Jr.	SK3C	V6
JONES, Isaac L.	S2C	V6S
JONES, William M.	S1 SM	V6
KEA, Thomas J.	F2C	V6
KELLY, Charles T.	RM3C	V6

KERR, Charles A.	GM2C	V6
KIEFFER, Linden H., Jr.	S1 QM	V6
LABYZON, Theopelius	F2 MOM	V6S
LEE, James V.	GM3C	V6
LOMAX, Edward	S1C	V6
LUSTER, Roosevelt	F1 MOM	V6
Mc KAY, Ira	S2C	V6
Mc MILLAN, Wendell P.	RM2C	V6
MATHIS, Alfred G.	RM3C	V6
MATHIS, Benjamin T.	SF2C	V6
MERRIWEATHER, J. A.	COX	V6
MOHN, Daniel A., Jr.	EM3C	V6S
MOORE, Johnnie	S1C	V6
MOSELY, Lee Otjice	EM3C	V6
MURRAY, John M.	STM2C	V6S
NANCE, Clarence A.	EM2C	V6
NAVRATIL, Elmer A.	BM1C	USN
OGLESHY, Theodore R.	F2 MOM	V6
OXTON, George Wilmot	CGMA	USN
PATTERSON, J. P.	Y3C	V6
PATUS, Charles John	MOMM1C	O1
PEARSON, John L.	MOMM2C	V6
PENNY, Frank L.	CM2C	V6
PERKINS, Arnold B.	S1C	V6S
POTTER, Deamos	COX	V6
PUGH, Edward	S2C	V6
PURCE, Howard V.	S2RDM	V6S
REDMOND, William L.	MOMM2C	V6
REED, Ernest C.	S2C	V6S
REEVES, Harry	F2 MM	V6S
REMBERT, William	S2C	V6
RHOADES, Richard S.	S2C	V6
RICE, Leslie J.	CK1C	USN
RIVERS, Francis E.	S1C	V6
ROBINSON, Leonard E.	F1C	V6
RORIE, Roger W.	S1C	V6S
St. JAMES, Carl R.	F1 MOM	V6S
SAUNDERS, Harold B.	S1C	V6
SAUNDERS, Robert B.	MOMM2C	V6
SHELTON, Felix	STM2c	V6S

SHORES, James N.	Y2C	V6
SIMMONS, Walter E.	F1 MOM	V6
SIMS, James W.	MOMM3C	V6
SINGLETON, Luke	S2RDM	V6S
SMILEY, Frank V.	S2C	V6
SMITH, Emmanuel R.	S2C	V6
SMITH, George E., Jr.	EM3C	V6
SMITH, Theodore R.	EM2C	V6
SMITH, William H., Jr.	MOMM2C	V6
SPENCER, Howard R.	MM2C	V6
STEVENS, Leroy G.	CEMA	V6
STEVENSON, Jethro W.	S1C	V6
TAYLOR, James, Jr.	RM3C	V6
TAYLOR, James E.	STM2C	V6S
TEBBETTS, Edward L.	CYA	V6
THOMAS, Jimmy L.	F2C	V6
THOMPSON, Calvin L.	S2C	V6S
TICFSON, James H.	S2C	V6S
TURNER, John C.	MOMM2C	V6
VINCENT, Warren N.	GM2C	V6
WALKER, Charles A.	S2C	V6
WALKER, James E.	S2C	V6S
WALZAK, Peter B.	CCSP	F4D
WEBSTER, Amos	MOMM3C	V6
WHITE, Mozell	S2C	IND
WILBURN, F. J., Jr.	SC3C	V6
WILLIAMS, David O.	M1C	V6
WILLIAMS, Homer Leo	MM1C	USN
WILLIAMS, Sullivan	S1C	V6
WILSON, Robert L.	S1C	V6S
WITHAM, Francis E.	BM2C	USN
WOLK, Louis N.	CBM(PA)	USNR
WOOD, Frank	GM3C	V6
WOOD, James	EM3C	V6
WRIGHT, James S.	EM2C	V6
YOUNG, Albert	S1C	V6

Index

About the Author

Mary Pat Kelly is an award-winning author and filmmaker whose unique background combines academic achievement, popular entertainment, and public service. She received her doctorate in English—with a concentration in film and Irish literature—from the City University of New York Graduate School in 1982. She has taught at Brooklyn College and City College and guest lectured at numerous other colleges, including Williams and the U.S. Military Academy.

Dr. Kelly's film credits include screenwriting for both Paramount Pictures and Columbia Pictures, as well as writing and producing for such popular television shows as *The Dick Cavett Show, Good Morning America,* and *Saturday Night Live.* Her documentary for Public Television *To Live for Ireland* (1987) was nominated for an Emmy and won the special jury award at the San Francisco Film Festival. The author's first published book, *Martin Scorsese: A Journey* (1991), was a critical and commercial success in the United States and on the best-seller list in Britain.

Dr. Kelly produced and directed *Home Away from Home: The Yanks in Ireland,* which was introduced by Walter Cronkite and broadcast on the PBS network in 1994. Her book by the same name was published by Appletree Press.

Proudly We Served is the basis for a PBS documentary directed by Dr. Kelly. A feature film is in the works.

The **Naval Institute Press** is the book-publishing arm of the U.S. Naval Institute, a private, nonprofit society for sea service professionals and others who share an interest in naval and maritime affairs. Established in 1873 at the U.S. Naval Academy in Annapolis, Maryland, where its offices remain, today the Naval Institute has more than 100,000 members worldwide.

Members of the Naval Institute receive the influential monthly magazine *Proceedings* and discounts on fine nautical prints and on ship and aircraft photos. They also have access to the transcripts of the Institute's Oral History Program and get discounted admission to any of the Institute-sponsored seminars offered around the country.

The Naval Institute also publishes *Naval History* magazine. This colorful bimonthly is filled with entertaining and thought-provoking articles, first-person reminiscences, and dramatic art and photography. Members receive a discount on *Naval History* subscriptions.

The Naval Institute's book-publishing program, begun in 1898 with basic guides to naval practices, has broadened its scope in recent years to include books of more general interest. Now the Naval Institute Press publishes more than seventy titles each year, ranging from how-to books on boating and navigation to battle histories, biographies, ship and aircraft guides, and novels. Institute members receive discounts on the Press's nearly 400 books in print.

For a free catalog describing Naval Institute Press books currently available, and for further information about subscribing to *Naval History* magazine or about joining the U.S. Naval Institute, please write to:

Membership & Communications Department
U.S. Naval Institute
118 Maryland Avenue
Annapolis, Maryland 21402-5035
Or call, toll-free, (800) 233-USNI.

MARTIN SHEERIN

MARY PAT KELLY is an award-winning author and filmmaker whose unique background combines academic achievement, popular entertainment, and public service. She received her doctorate in English—with a concentration in film and Irish literature—from the City University of New York Graduate School in 1982. She has taught at Brooklyn College and City College and guest lectured at numerous other colleges, including Williams and the U.S. Military Academy.

Dr. Kelly's film credits include screenwriting for both Paramount Pictures and Columbia Pictures, as well as writing and producing for such popular television shows as *Good Morning America, The Dick Cavett Show*, and *Saturday Night Live*. Her documentary *To Live for Ireland* (1987) was nominated for an Emmy. Her interest in the men of the *Mason* evolved from a documentary she produced in 1992 on American servicemen in Northern Ireland in World War II. The author's book *Martin Scorsese: A Journey* (1991) was well received in the United States and on the bestseller list in Britain. Her most recent book, *Home Away from Home: The Yanks in Ireland*, was published in 1994 by Appletree Press. Dr. Kelly lives with her husband, photographer Martin Sheerin, on New York City's Upper West Side.